About This Book

Why is this topic important?

Often beginning trainers, course developers and subject matter experts (SMEs) design a training program based on past experience and without formal training. To go beyond the basics, trainers, course designers and SMEs need additional skills to develop learning activities and training materials to reach learning objectives. Although many books exist about how to design training programs, few address how to simplify writing and developing learning activities. This book helps simplify a complex process and speed materials development.

What can you achieve with this book?

Successful training programs are designed using a series of interactive materials that help learners discover concepts and apply what is learned back to the job. The systematic process described will help raise the trainer's skills to the next level of development. Easy to use tools and templates answer all the questions trainers, course designers, and SMEs may have about how to develop training materials and more easily create the best training program in the shortest amount of time.

How is this book organized?

Each chapter begins with objectives to help trainers identify what new skills and insights can move their training beyond the basics and help them to develop effective training materials. The tools in each chapter are provided on the book's website for customizing and duplication. Each tool is in a Word file for easy access and customization for your use.

Each chapter discusses a learning method, breaks it down into supporting parts and shows the trainer how to write successful learning activities for that method. Examples of each learning method are provided. Learning methods include simulations and games, case studies, inventories, tests, role plays, demonstrations, and how to develop visuals to support each learning activity.

About Pfeiffer

Pfeiffer serves the professional development and hands-on resource needs of training and human resource practitioners and gives them products to do their jobs better. We deliver proven ideas and solutions from experts in HR development and HR management, and we offer effective and customizable tools to improve workplace performance. From novice to seasoned professional, Pfeiffer is the source you can trust to make yourself and your organization more successful.

Essential Knowledge Pfeiffer produces insightful, practical, and comprehensive materials on topics that matter the most to training and HR professionals. Our Essential Knowledge resources translate the expertise of seasoned professionals into practical, how-to guidance on critical workplace issues and problems. These resources are supported by case studies, worksheets, and job aids and are frequently supplemented with CD-ROMs, websites, and other means of making the content easier to read, understand, and use.

Essential Tools Pfeiffer's Essential Tools resources save time and expense by offering proven, ready-to-use materials—including exercises, activities, games, instruments, and assessments—for use during a training or team-learning event. These resources are frequently offered in looseleaf or CD-ROM format to facilitate copying and customization of the material.

Pfeiffer also recognizes the remarkable power of new technologies in expanding the reach and effectiveness of training. While e-hype has often created whizbang solutions in search of a problem, we are dedicated to bringing convenience and enhancements to proven training solutions. All our e-tools comply with rigorous functionality standards. The most appropriate technology wrapped around essential content yields the perfect solution for today's on-the-go trainers and human resource professionals.

Pfeiffer
www.pfeiffer.com

Essential resources for training and HR professionals

Pfeiffer™
A Wiley Brand

HOW TO WRITE TERRIFIC TRAINING MATERIALS

Methods, Tools, and Techniques

Jean Barbazette

WILEY

Author photo by Mike Gilmore
Cover design: Wiley
Cover images: (hand typing) © Fotosearch/Getty RF; (checklist) © Daniel Kulinski/Getty RF; (hand writing) © Guido
    Mieth/Getty RF

Library of Congress Cataloging-in-Publication Data

Library of Congress Cataloging-in-Publication Data has been applied for and is on file with the Library of Congress.

ISBN 978-1-118-45403-9 (paper); ISBN 978-1-118-58374-6 (ebk.);
ISBN 978-1-118-58382-1 (ebk.); ISBN 978-1-118-58383-8 (ebk.)

Acquiring Editor: Matthew Davis
Director of Development: Kathleen Dolan Davies
Developmental Editor: Susan Rachmeler
Production Editor: Michael Kay

Editor: Rebecca Taff
Indexer: Sylvia Coates
Editorial Assistant: Ryan Noll
Manufacturing Supervisor: Becky Morgan

Printed in the United States of America
PB Printing   10 9 8 7 6 5 4 3 2 1

For Richard

Contents

Exhibits and Tools

Website Contents

All of the tools in this book are available at a Premium Content Website. Here is the link and password to access these tools:

URL: www.pfeiffer.com/go/barbazette
password: professional

Tools

Acknowledgments

Every author has many people to thank, those who provided suggestions, ideas, critiques and contributions to complete the book. Thanks to Maria Chilcote and Melissa Smith, managing partners of The Training Clinic. Thanks to Linda Ernst, Judy Robb, Hans Brouwer, Jenn Labin, Insoo Kim, and Roberta Olden. Thanks to all the folks at Pfeiffer who have improved this book, including Lisa Shannon, Matt Davis, Ryan Noll, Michael Kay, Rebecca Taff, and Sylvia Coates.

Introduction

Purpose

This book is intended to help trainers move their training and course development skills to the next level. How to *facilitate* each of the training methods described in my previous book, *The Art of Great Training Delivery*, is clearly explained for the course developer. This book addresses how to *write and develop* a variety of training activities to create the best learning experience and improve learner retention. In my previous book, *Training Needs Assessment*, I end with how to write a training plan. This book picks up where these two previous works ended.

Audience

This book was written for the trainer who wants to move beyond basic training skills and become a course designer and materials developer. Although the main target audience is the "intermediate" trainer, new trainers with little classroom experience and SMEs can benefit from the tools provided here.

Product Description

Chapters 1 and 2 present an overview of the design process and how to plan to develop materials. Chapter 3 helps you look at the writing process. Chapter 4 offers several nifty tools to develop training materials. Chapter 5 offers suggestions about writing and adapting materials. Chapters 6, 7, 8, and 9 delve into writing specific training materials based on the learning objective. Chapters 10, 11, and 12 round out the writing process by looking at developing tests, lesson plans, and audiovisuals. A glossary, bibliography, and index are included. This book is the sixth volume in a series of train-the-trainer books by Jean Barbazette available from Pfeiffer, an Imprint of Wiley.

Overview of the Design Process

This chapter will help the developer to:

- Identify essential steps in the training design process
- Locate where materials development fits into the design process
- Use a ten-part training plan as the blueprint for materials development
- Present the plan to management and gain approval

Exhibit

- 1.1. Three Phases of Design

Essential Steps in the Training Design Process

Designing a training program usually takes three phases: planning, development, and evaluation and revision. See Exhibit 1.1 for a picture of the three phases. Typically, a decision to develop a new training program comes from the installation of new equipment, changes in a process or procedure, or as the result of a performance deficiency.

Phase One, planning, begins with an evaluation of a person's or group's performance accompanied by interviews and observations. Review a job description to be sure it is current, and also review job standards. Through these observations, develop a task analysis to describe the appropriate way to complete a task. Write a target population analysis to identify what you know about this group. Write course objectives and decide whether there are prerequisites to attending this course and how you will evaluate whether the course participants meet these prerequisites. Create a strategy to decide how you will evaluate whether course objectives are met and whether the training course you are about to design will meet the business need that prompted course development. Summarize all the planning information in a ten-part training plan, described later in the chapter.

Phase Two, development, begins with writing a broad content outline of the essential elements that will help the learner meet the course's objectives. Next, identify the appropriate sequence of content elements. Flush out and refine the content and identify learning methods that are appropriate for this target population. Determine the best sequence of the variety of learning methods. Develop learning activities, exercises, tests, and handout materials. If appropriate, write a script for supporting audiovisual materials and write a lesson plan. Pilot the class to determine whether the learning objectives, and therefore the business need, will be met from the course.

Phase Three, evaluation and revision, uses the four-level model created by Dr. Donald Kirkpatrick (1998): assess the reactions of the learners to the course; decide whether the learning objectives have been met through new knowledge, skills, and attitudes; identify whether new learning transferred to the job; and check whether bottom-line results are met.

Where Materials Development Fits into the Design Process

Materials development, or writing terrific training materials, occurs in Phase Two.

Exhibit 1.1. Three Phases of Design

1. Planning

Review performance evaluations

Conduct interviews and observations

Complete target population analysis

Determine course prerequisites

Identify prerequisite evaluation methods

Write a training plan

Review job description

Create or update job standards

Complete task analysis

Write course objectives

Strategize a means to evaluate methods

2. Development

Develop broad content outline

Refine content

Sequence methods

Evaluate the pacing of activities

Pilot course

Sequence and group broad content

Select methods

Develop learner activities, exercises, handouts, and tests

Complete lesson plan

3. Evaluation and Revision

Reaction of learners   Learning new knowledge, skills,
                                                       and attitudes

Transfer of new learning to job   Bottom-line results

A Ten-Part Training Plan to Use as a Blueprint for Materials Development[1]

Following the completion of one or more needs analyses and the steps in Phase One of the design process, a training plan is usually written to report the results of the analyses and to meet projected training needs for a group of employees (such as first-line supervisors) or for a period of time, such as for the coming year. Sometimes training plans are called performance improvement plans to demonstrate that more than training solutions are offered. A complete training plan often offers non-training solutions as well.

Here are the ten parts of a training plan, along with references to which type of analysis would develop each type of information.

1. Define the Issue

Define the issues that are related to a business need that training can address. For example, for either of the following issues it would be appropriate to develop a training plan.

- How can we successfully open ten new stores with the current skills of the assistant store managers who would be promoted to store manager?

- Middle managers have no advanced training beyond what they received when they became supervisors.

---

[1]Complete information for a training plan is in Chapter 10 of *Training Needs Assessment* ©2006 Jean Barbazette, reproduced by permission from Pfeiffer, an Imprint of Wiley.

Often the issues are identified by completing a *performance analysis*. Remember to offer non-training recommendations where appropriate.

2. Identify the Need

Some organizations become trapped into putting on training programs because they are popular or requested without regard for linking training to a business need. Often a request for time management, stress management, or communication skills indicates "needs" that ought to be sorted out from "wants." Identify how widespread the "need" or "want" is and whether or not it is related to job performance.

A *needs versus wants analysis* develops this type of information.

3. Contract with Supervisors

How will supervisors or managers of those attending training be included in the planning and follow-up for improved performance? Define the role of the supervisor or manager of the participants and identify how to prepare them to reinforce the training.

4. Identify/Establish Performance Standards

Often, training is requested to improve performance. Are there performance standards to use as the goal for a minimum level of acceptable performance? The operational area, not the training function, has to establish job performance standards. It becomes difficult to train if vague or no standards exist. ("Just make them more professional" is an example of a request that may or may not have an agreed-on standard of acceptable job performance.)

Information related to performance standards is developed from *job/task analysis, performance analysis, and goal analysis.*

5. Identify Trainees

Who is to be trained? What job classifications do they hold and how many people need training? *Target population analysis* develops this type of information.

6. Establish Training Objectives and Training Evaluation Criteria and Results

Decide how you will know the training was successful. How will learning and new skills be evaluated? How will you tie training to bottom-line results and back to the business need that dictates the training?

This information is developed by conducting a *performance analysis and needs versus wants analysis.*

7. Determine the Cost of Training

What are the costs to assess the need for training, design the training, develop learner and instructor materials, present the training, and evaluate the training? Are the costs worth the benefit?

A *feasibility analysis* develops this type of information.

8. Select/Develop the Training Program

Decide whether you will present an existing program or buy a packaged training program. Decide whether you will use internal subject-matter experts as developers/trainers or hire an external consultant, designer, or trainer. No needs analysis tool is used to answer this question completely.

Perhaps a *contextual analysis* can answer some of the issues around program selection.

9. Schedule the Training

What time of the day, week, month, quarter, or year is best for this type of training? What are the consequences of training "on the clock" or on the employees' own time in your organization?

Contextual analysis develops this type of information.

10. Evaluate the Results

Apply the criteria using these four levels and objectives from Number 6 above:

- Participant reaction (measured in the classroom or in an online survey following training)
- Learning (measured in the classroom)

- Job performance (measured in the workplace)
- Results (based on the business need identified in Number 1)

How to Present a Training Plan to Management and Gain Approval

How a training plan is presented to management (or to the client) to gain approval depends on the decision-making process in each organization. If the internal client who requested a training plan or some type of needs assessment is the management decision-maker, ask the client what type of information he or she needs to make a decision. What amount of discussion and detail is sought? Does the client prefer to see a summary of data or both a summary and raw data from which the summary is drawn? Does the client prefer to make decisions from the data or to select from recommendations made by the trainer conducting the needs analyses?

Since most training plans are complex, it is helpful to provide a one-page overview and allow time to read the plan prior to discussing it. Provide a copy of the plan to managers at least a week before the meeting to discuss the plan along with a proposed agenda or questions for discussion. Most plans need some additional explanation and discussion before budgetary approval is given.

Often, presenting parts of the training plan visually can help clarify what is or is not a part of a training plan.

Next Steps

The presentation of a training plan is both an ending of one process and the beginning of another. Once decisions are made from the training plan, identify who will follow up on those decisions. How will this information be handed off to the course developer? How will management inform the target population of the training and non-training solutions selected to address the performance issues? Who will coordinate and implement the decisions made from the training plan?

This book will address the development of training materials listed in Phase Two of the design process.

Objectives for Writing Projects

This chapter will help the developer to:

- Develop instructional objectives versus objectives for training program materials
- Write instructional objectives that benefit course designers, trainers, and learners
- Develop writing objectives with four characteristics
- Learn four elements of well-written objectives for training program materials
- Review sample objectives for writing projects

Exhibit

- 2.1. Behavioral Verbs

Tool

- 2.1. Writing Training Materials Objectives Template

Instructional Objectives Versus Objectives for Training Program Materials

Most course developers are familiar with instructional objectives. A brief review of the characteristics of well-written instructional objectives follows. Trainers who write training materials need to use objectives with similar characteristics. Following the presentation of *instructional* objectives is a discussion of well-written objectives for *training program materials,* with examples of objectives for writing three types of program materials.

Write Instructional Objectives

Instructional objectives describe what the learner will be able to do at the end of the training. It is an expression of the desired result of the learning experience, a statement of the desired outcome. Instructional objectives have several purposes:

- Specifically identify the learner's role and what the learner is to do
- Provide a means for measuring learning
- Focus and narrow the content
- Help clarify expectations to ensure they are realistic and achievable
- Communicate to the instructor and the learner what is expected
- Market the benefits of training to learners and others
- Identify methods, media and/or activities needed to reach the objective

Four Characteristics of Instructional Objectives

Well-developed instructional objectives have four characteristics. They:

1. Are written from the learner's point of view
2. Use specific behavioral verbs that describe performance
3. Give a condition or circumstance under which the behavior is done
4. State the minimum level of achievement

Here is an example: Given the necessary equipment and the procedure manual [this is the condition], the learner [written from the learner's point of view] will repair a digital cell telephone [specific behavioral verb] within 45 minutes [minimum level of achievement].

Look more closely at these four characteristics and why each is important to a well-written objective. The objective is written from the learner's point of view because that is the only way the trainer knows the learner understands the lesson. If the objective is written from the trainer's point of view, success is more difficult to measure, or the activity can become meaningless. For example, if the previous example were written from the trainer's point of view, it might state that the trainer will explain how to repair a digital cell telephone. There is no way to measure the learner's success, which is the point of the training session.

Using specific behavioral words can be a challenge. Sometimes trainers use the verbs "know," "understand," or "appreciate," which makes it difficult to measure results. How do you know the learner "understood"? If the learner can *identify* the five steps to repair a telephone, use that more specific verb. Exhibit 2.1 is a list of several behavioral words to help you write specific objectives. Verbs are divided into three categories: skill, attitude, and knowledge.

Exhibit 2.1. Behavioral Verbs

Skill Verbs

advise	aid	alert
approve	arrange	assist
balance	calculate	calibrate
change	check	choose
coach	conduct	contain
copy	decide	delegate
deliver	demonstrate	design
develop	diagnose	direct
distribute	examine	execute

expand	facilitate	follow
generate	guide	help
install	invent	isolate
join	launch	lead
level	listen	lubricate
maintain	manage	mandate
match	measure	mediate
moderate	modify	monitor
operate	order	participate
perform	present	prevent
produce	program	qualify
record	regulate	remove
request	select	simulate
synchronize	trim	troubleshoot
use	weigh	

Attitude Verbs

adapt	agree	appreciate
challenge	comply	convince
ensure	harmonize	instigate
interpret	judge	prevail
stretch	suggest	sustain

Knowledge Verbs

adjust	analyze	apply
ascertain	assess	assign
categorize	classify	communicate
compare	concentrate	confer
deliberate	describe	detect
determine	discriminate	discuss
educate	establish	evaluate
explain	figure	file
frame	identify	improve
initiate	instruct	interpret
learn	observe	organize

originate	paraphrase	plan
prepare	prioritize	read
recall	recognize	remember
remind	resolve	retain
review	revise	schedule
specify	state	survey
synthesize	translate	
verbalize	verify	

The third characteristic of an appropriately written learning objective is to describe the condition that must exist for the learner to perform and without which the learner could not perform the task. The condition can be stated as what is given/allowed or denied. Examples are

What is given or allowed?

- Resources, information

- Tools and equipment, references

- Assistance from another person

What is denied?

- From memory

- Without references

- Alone

The fourth characteristic of an appropriately written learning objective is to describe the minimum level of achievement, or usually how well the learner should use information or be able to perform. To be effective, these criteria must be measurable and tied to performance standards. Levels of achievement can be stated in one of three ways:

- Quality (how well)

- Quantity (how many)

- Speed (how fast)

Here are some sample learning objectives. Some of these objectives are complete examples and contain all four characteristics of an instructional objective. Some are incomplete examples and do not contain all four characteristics. Can you identify what's missing from the incomplete examples? Correct answers are on the following page.

At the end of the workshop the participants will be able to:

1. Given a current ATM account and ATM machine, withdraw $40 from a checking account.

2. Without references, describe the situations for the use of safety glasses.

3. Identify the approved exit routes to be used during a fire.

4. Given the recipes, the equipment, and the necessary ingredients, cook a dinner that meets the requirements of a gourmet meal within three hours.

5. Given a CD of Beethoven's symphonies, demonstrate appreciation of the construction of one of the pieces.

6. Given the necessary equipment and the procedure manual, repair a digital cell phone.

Four Elements of Well-Written Objectives for Training Program Materials

The previous information describes learning objectives for the participants. When a trainer develops training materials, the objectives for the trainer are similar. First, identify who is going to be the user of what you develop and what you want the user to do as a result of using your lesson plan, learner handout materials, tests, exercises, and activities and scripts.

There are four elements to consider when writing training program materials:

1. Who is the user? (Identify by job title or responsibility.)

2. What do you want the user to be able to do? (Use a behavioral action verb.)

Answers to the Objective Exercise

1. Given a current ATM account and ATM machine, withdraw $40 from a checking account. [correct]

2. Without references, describe the situations for the use of safety glasses. [The level of achievement is missing. It could be from memory or to list three situations.]

3. Identify the approved exit routes to be used during a fire. [The condition is missing. It could be, given a floor plan for this building.]

4. Given the recipes, the equipment, and the necessary ingredients, cook a dinner that meets the requirements of a gourmet meal within three hours. [correct]

5. Given a CD of Beethoven's symphonies, demonstrate appreciation of the construction of one of the pieces. [correct]

6. Given the necessary equipment and the procedure manual, repair a digital cell phone. [Level of achievement is missing. Add a quality measure or how well the repair must be done.]

3. What is the condition or circumstance for the use of the materials? (What is given or denied while developing the materials?)

4. What is the level of achievement for the use of the materials? (Identify quality, quantity, or speed for the use of the materials.)

Sample Objectives for Writing Materials

Examples of Objectives for Writing Lesson Plans

- The teller trainer will introduce paying and receiving concepts through lecture and demonstration activities so the new teller can identify any type of paying and receiving activity in a role-play setting.

- The experienced teller will demonstrate the paying and receiving activities so the new teller will be able to perform any type of paying and receiving transaction when dealing with real customers.

Examples of Objectives for Writing Learner Handout Materials, Tests, Exercises, and Activities

- The experienced customer service representatives will be able to complete the new order form correctly within 5 minutes.

- Using the invoice number record log, the accounts receivable clerk will assign a new invoice number in the appropriate category that does not duplicate other numbers.

Examples of Objectives for Writing Scripts (Objective Is Written for the Learner/Viewer, Not the Producer)

- After attending a PowerPoint presentation about the new cosmetic line for the coming season, the cosmetic clerk will be able to describe the intended customer for each product and how each product is to be used.

- After viewing the time management video, the manager will be able to identify three personal techniques to prioritize activities and eliminate time-wasters.

See Tool 2.1 for a template to write objectives to develop materials.

Tool 2.1. Writing Training Materials Objectives Template

What type of training materials will you develop?

❑ Lesson plan

❑ Exercise

❑ Case study

❑ Other activity

❑ Test

❑ Script

There are four elements for objectives to write training materials. Fill the elements for your project below:

1. Who is the user? (Identify by job title or responsibility.)

2. What do you want the user to be able to do? (Use a behavioral action verb.)

3. What is the condition or circumstance for the use of the materials? (What is given or denied while developing the materials?

4. What is the level of achievement for the use of the materials? (Identify quality, quantity, or speed for the use of the materials.)

Next Steps

After you have written objective(s) for your writing project, you begin the writing process. Chapter 3 gives you an opportunity to assess your current skill in writing, as well as some suggestions to brainstorm and organize your ideas and overcome writer's block.

Use the Writing Process

This chapter will help the developer to:

- Assess his or her writing skills
- Use four steps to organize ideas
- Review different methods to brainstorm ideas before writing
- Use one of ten approaches to sequence ideas
- Edit what's been written
- Assess readability of materials

Exhibit

- 3.1. Mind Map Example

Tool

- 3.1. Brainstorming Template

Assess Your Writing Skills

Instructions: This quick assessment focuses on your writing skills, organization, clarity, and efficiency in the writing process. Then you are asked about your skill in developing four different types of training materials. Assess your skill in each of the areas by placing an "O" on the continuum to indicate your current skill level and an "X" for where you want to be.

Organization: To what extent do your materials have a solid structure and logical sequence?

I'm very disorganized.   I'm about average.   I'm very well organized.

Clarity: How often do learners follow-up to ask: "What did you mean by that?"

| I'm very foggy | I'm sometimes hard to read. | I'm so-so. | They get me on second readings | I'm clear. |

Efficiency: To what extent is the time you spend in developing materials a reasonable investment for the results you get?

| I spend too much time. | I'd like to spend less time. | I can manage it. | It's not too bad. | I'm quite efficient. |

Comfort with Developing Materials: To what extent do you hate the development tasks—or love them?

| I hate it! | I try to avoid developing materials. | I can live with it. | Usually comfortable. | I sometimes volunteer. |

Learner Materials: What's your skill in writing learner materials (handouts, activities, exercises, case studies, etc.)?

| I need help to be better. | Lots of rewrites | Okay, but need to be better. | Pretty good | Outstanding; others steal from me. |

Tests/Assessments: What's your skill level?

Don't know where to begin	Okay, but a struggle	Easy to write

Lesson Plans: What's your skill in developing lesson plans?

Minimal	Okay, but it takes a lot of time	Good overall	Easy to do effective plans

Audiovisual Scripts/PowerPoint: What's your skill level?

Basic	Intermediate	Advanced

The rest of this chapter will help you increase your organization, clarity, efficiency and comfort with the writing process. Later chapters will help you with four types of writing projects.

Use Four Steps to Organize Your Ideas

The first step to better organization of your ideas is to start with a learning objective, as described in Chapter 2. The objective is what drives the materials development process.

The second step to better organization of your ideas is to describe *what* needs to be developed. This is where content brainstorming is especially useful. There are a couple of ways to create comprehensive content: making a list (a left-brained, linear approach) and mind-mapping (a right-brained, non-linear approach). Both methods are effective if done well, using common "rules of brainstorming." These include:

- Go for quantity
- No editing
- Build on existing ideas

- Keep asking what comes next

- No bad ideas, suspend judgment

- Take risks

- Stop making excuses

- Take turns; encourage others

- Save discussion for later

- Write ideas so everyone can see contributions

Tool 3.1 shows the linear format to brainstorm content ideas. With this format, first free-write your ideas. Then go back and sequence them, crossing out items to stick to what the user needs.

Exhibit 3.1 shows a mind map format to brainstorm content ideas. With this format, ideas are written down and the relationship of one idea to another is indicated by its placement.

Exhibit 3.1. Mind Map Example

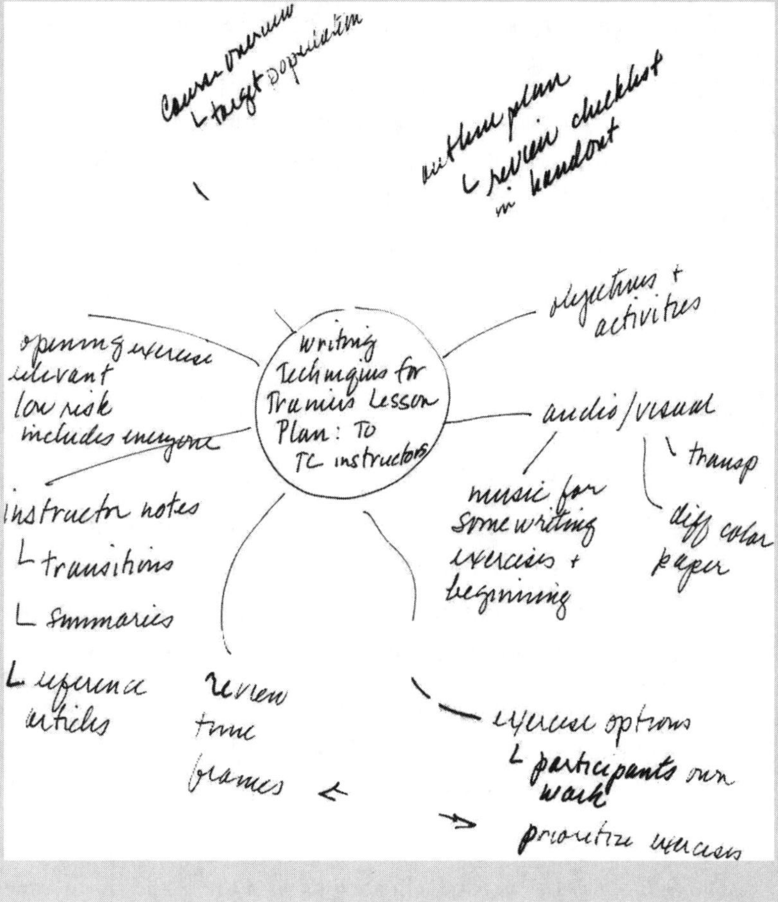

The third step to better organization of your ideas is to consider options for sequencing the information. Ten options are defined here:

1. *Psychological* sequencing presents the most acceptable ideas to the reader first and places the least acceptable ideas last. For example, describe the success and increased sales for the top-selling product and then list the techniques to build future sales of the lower-selling products.

2. *Chronological* or *historical* sequencing starts with the oldest ideas first and places the newest ideas last. *Reverse chronological*

sequencing starts with the newest ideas and traces their origin in history and ends with the oldest ideas. For example, during a new employee orientation session, the founding of the company is stated first and then acquisitions that built the company are listed in historical order.

3. *Job task or function* sequence starts with an overview of a job and lists the steps of completing a task or function in the order in which each task is completed. For example, describe the process for employees to safely lift heavy boxes.

4. *Familiar to unfamiliar* sequencing starts with an idea or content with which the reader is familiar and builds to newer or unfamiliar information. For example, describe the updated software for accounting clerks by first listing the steps that are familiar and then describing the changes to the process.

5. *Geographical* sequencing starts with one location and moves to the next location in one direction. For example, when describing an organization's multiple offices, start with the home office location in New York and list the additional offices from east to west.

6. *Cause-to-effect* sequencing begins with the initial incident and builds to the result of specific actions. For example, placing a heat source near combustible materials caused a fire that burned down a building.

7. *Effect-to-cause* sequencing begins with the result or outcome and traces ideas or events back to the cause. For example, the current deficit in the budget is traced back to overspending in five budget categories.

8. *Stimulus-response* sequencing begins with an action and identifies the likely outcome. For example, when the telephone rings, the telephone is answered.

9. *Size* sequencing starts with the largest and ends with the smallest. The reverse can also be used by starting with the smallest unit and ending with the largest. For example, shipping boxes offered by the

postal service include six sizes holding twenty-five pounds and ending with one pound.

10. *Organizational unit* sequencing is a way of describing an organizational chart that begins with the top of the organization (CEO and board of directors) and shows a reporting structure to the bottom of the organization (line manufacturing workers).

Whatever sequence you choose, be sure to share the sequence plan with the learner because it makes it easier to follow your logic and learn more quickly.

The fourth step to better organization of your ideas is to write your ideas. This is a three-part process itself!

First, you *must* open with a statement of purpose. This takes the form of a business need, a benefit to the reader, or what outcome can be reached. For example, here is a statement of purpose for a selling skills training video:

This video demonstrates how the new accounts representative can successfully sell a money market account. New accounts representatives often think of selling as order taking or something that used car salespeople do. This video is meant to be an attractive and easy-to-follow model of the four steps to the sale, illustrating listening and questioning skills, including how to handle an objection. The four steps include:

1. Identify the customer's need.
2. Sell the features and benefits of the right product.
3. Close the sale.
4. Explain how to cross-sell additional products.

Second, free-write each idea. Using the brainstormed list or mind map as a guide, write what you know about each idea. Ignore the compulsion to edit, use proper grammar, and spell correctly for now. If you know you've made a mistake, just circle it or highlight it, leave space for a later revision, and keep going. Don't fix it now.

If you're having writer's block, try pretending you're talking to a friend and write down what you would say. Often times, I write materials that

I have taught in the past, so standing up and pretending I'm in front of a group helps me find the words that I would say to a group of learners.

Third, edit your free-write materials. Read what you have written and complete a "big picture revision." What is the style or tone of what you have written? Is the style or tone consistent? What format changes need to be considered? Next, complete "what's the point" revisions by focusing on the clarity of your message. Can you be more concise or simplify what and how you present your ideas? Finally, complete a "detail" revision by checking grammar, spelling, and punctuation. Microsoft Word and other word processing software have spelling and grammar tools.

To determine the readability of what you have written, use a tool like the Gunning Fog Index. Using a one-hundred-word sample, count the number of words and divide by the number of sentences. Average sentence length of fourteen to sixteen words results in standard readability. Count the number of syllables in a one-hundred-word sample. One hundred fifty syllables per one hundred words denotes standard readability. The longer the sentence length and the greater the number of syllables, the fewer the number of readers who can read and understand your meaning on the first reading.

To test the readability of your copy and learn more about the Gunning Fog Index, see www.readabilityformulas.com.

Tool 3.1. Brainstorming Template

Sequence	Free-write your ideas here.

Next Steps

Now that you have assessed your writing skills and determined how to create a basic outline of the content of learning materials, decide how to create materials using the best learning methods. The next chapter contains several tools and exhibits that provide a foundation of learning principles to help you write any type of learning materials.

4

What Are the Best Training Methods?

This chapter will help the developer to:

- Select the best learning experiences
- Select the appropriate technical training methods to promote recall and application
- Select the best audiovisual support for materials design and delivery
- Pace training methods to avoid boredom
- Determine how much practice is needed to acquire a skill
- Sequence training methods using a situational training model
- Describe how the materials development process changes based on classroom versus e-learning delivery

Tools

- 4.1. Best Learning Experiences
- 4.2. Technical Training Methods to Promote Recall
- 4.3. Technical Training Methods to Promote Application
- 4.4. Select the Best Audiovisual Support

- 4.5. Methods Variety Scale
- 4.6. DIF: How Much Practice and Training?
- 4.7. Situational Training Methods Model

Exhibits

- 4.1. Tools to Promote Interaction
- 4.2. Materials and Other Logistics
- 4.3. Connect with the Virtual Learner
- 4.4. Compensate for Lack of Face-to-Face Contact

In this chapter we will cover methods you can use to help adults remember what they learned in training.

For your training to be effective, consider using a variety of training methods that best meet a learning objective. A variety of methods helps appeal to different learning styles. Most adults learn best when they are actively involved in their learning experiences. When learners discover concepts, rather than listen to them in a lecture or video, retention improves. When a variety of learning methods are logically sequenced, the learners' attention and retention improve. This chapter addresses these issues using tools and examples you can adapt for your training sessions. These tools will build a foundation for writing training materials. How to write activities using these methods will be discussed in later chapters.

Select the Best Learning Experiences

Selecting the best training method is easy when you first identify the learning objective. Remember, learning objectives are written from the learner's point of view. For example, *by the end of this session, the new sales representatives will identify the features and benefits of our new product.* In order to reach this objective, sales representatives will need to remember product knowledge information. The most common training method to impart knowledge is to give a lecture. However, there are several other options, such as a demonstration, video, information search, interview, reading printed materials, and tests that can also meet this learning objective.

Tool 4.1 is a table that identifies the best technique or learning experience to achieve the learning objective. In the table, the name of the training technique is to the left. The middle column describes the technique from the learners' point of view. The right column tells what type of objective is best reached by using this technique. "K" indicates a knowledge objective, for learning facts, theories, or visual identification. "S" indicates an objective that teaches a mental or physical skill and includes analyzing or applying facts, principles, and concepts, or performing a perceptual or motor skill. "A" stands for influencing the learners' attitudes, opinions, and motivations. Some techniques are best used to teach only one type of objective. Other techniques can be used effectively to teach more than one.

Tool 4.1. Best Learning Experiences[1]

Technique	Description (Written from the learners' perspective)	Best Use		
		K	S	A
Application Sharing	Share the instructor's screen and perform functions; can attend a cyber tour of the Internet	X	X	X
Behavior Modeling	See a model or ideal enactment of desired behavior demonstrated by instructor or video	X		X
Case Study or Scenario	Analyze and solve a problem, a case situation, or a scenario, alone and/or in a small group	X	X	X
Demonstration	Hear the instructor verbally explain and see the instructor perform a procedure or process	X		X
Discussion or "Chat"	Discuss issues, share ideas and opinions in a live group or by posting in a threaded discussion	X	X	X
Discussion, Inquiry Oriented	Participate in a discussion where the facilitator asks planned questions to encourage discovery learning	X		X
Field Trip, Observation, Cyber-trip	Experience or view actual situations for first-hand observation and study or viewing websites through a browser	X		
Film, Video or Skit	View a one-way organized presentation	X		X
Flip Chart, White Board	See the instructor and or learners list items brainstormed or discussed; make drawings	X		X
Games, Exercises, Structured Experiences	Participate in planned activities, then discuss feelings, reactions, and application to real life	X	X	X
In Basket Exercises	Review typical paperwork to sort, delay, discard, or act on immediately	X	X	X
Information Search	Search for information in source materials alone or in a group	X	X	

[1]Special thanks to Melissa Smith, managing partner of The Training Clinic, who helped create this chart. Reprinted from *The Art of Great Training Delivery*, © 2006 by Jean Barbazette. Reproduced by permission of Pfeiffer, an Imprint of Wiley. www.pfeiffer.com.

Technique	Description (Written from the learners' perspective)	Best Use K	S	A
Interview	Question a resource person on behalf of the audience	X	X	X
Jigsaw Learning or Teaching Learning Team	Study groups concentrate on different information; members re-form in groups to teach each other	X	X	X
Learning Tournament	Review material, then compete against other study groups in self-scoring test	X		
Lecture	Listen to a one-way presentation of information	X		
Polling	Respond to a variety of choices through selecting or sequencing choices	X	X	X
Practice or Return Demonstration	Repeat performance of a skill under supervision of instructor, and then again without supervision		X	
Printed Resources	Use charts, posters, laminated job aids, cards, and handouts for reference or as a resource	X		X
Role Playing or Skill Practice	Dramatize a problem or situation, then follow with discussion		X	X
Self-Assessment or Inventory	Examine own values, skills, style, etc., through experiences, surveys, and activities	X		X
Simulations	Experience a situation as nearly real as possible, followed by discussion		X	X
Study Groups	Read material individually, then clarify content in small groups	X		X
Task Force Project	Groups generate plans that can be used in the actual work situation to solve a real problem	X	X	X
Teaching Project	Learners teach new information or skills to one another	X	X	
Tests	Answer questions or complete activities that test comprehension, recall, application, etc., of the learning material	X	X	
Writing Tasks	Reflects on own understanding of and response to training, usually descriptive – either planning to use skills or describing an event.	X	X	X

To continue with the example of the sales representatives, after learning features and benefits of a new product, additional objectives can develop further learning. For example, *sales representatives will match product benefits to five different types of customers.* Since this objective requires skill application, look for training techniques that have an "X" in the "S" column. The best learning experiences might involve a case study, a small group discussion about different types of customers, and matching benefits to each customer's needs. A role play or simulation of a customer interview will also help meet this objective.

Following are two additional training situations. After you read through each situation and the suggested learning objectives, categorize each learning objective as a knowledge, skill, or attitude objective using Tool 4.1, and then identify at least three training techniques that would help these learners meet their objectives.

Situation One

An experienced cashier, Pamela, has been moved from hardware to children's shoes in a very large department store. From previous training sessions, you remember Pamela as an eager learner who by now is familiar with store policies and cashiering procedures. She is used to dealing with home repair enthusiasts and decorators (adults). Now she must deal with different customers and different merchandise.

Your learning objectives for Pamela's first week in children's shoes are for her to:

1. Learn the new merchandise so she can make appropriate recommendations

2. Develop different strategies to deal with children and their parents

Suggested Answers

The first objective is for Pamela to acquire knowledge about the new merchandise. Pamela can achieve this objective by observing existing employees, doing an information search to learn how the stock is organized, or reviewing printed resources and catalogs that describe the merchandise. The second objective is a skill based on a positive attitude of helping children and their parents find the right shoes. Case studies, discussions, and role play or skill practice can help Pamela reach this objective, since each of these methods addresses both skills and attitudes.

Situation Two

You are assigned to develop materials to train the new auxiliary volunteers at your hospital. During a previous class for the new volunteers, the only element not covered was responding to medical questions and handling sensitive or confidential information. You need to develop materials to include this information in your next class. Your objectives are to:

1. Distinguish sensitive and confidential information from information that can be discussed openly

2. Practice responding to questions about sensitive or confidential information

Suggested Answers

Distinguishing sensitive and confidential information from information that can be discussed openly is a knowledge objective. If you selected information search, case study, inquiry-oriented discussion, or interview, these techniques are good choices to reach this objective and let the learners discover the information. While giving a brief lecture might reach this objective, it could be the most boring alternative. The second objective requires skill to respond to medical questions. Responding to sensitive or confidential information is a skill that is guided by a gentle and caring attitude when speaking to patients or their family members. A combination of case studies, interviews, role plays, and tests can help the volunteers reach this objective.

So far the examples and objectives are about teaching "soft" skills, for which Tool 4.1 is well-suited. Tool 4.1 is also useful in selecting the best learning experiences for teaching technical topics. Tool 4.2 and Tool 4.3 are also helpful for selecting techniques to teach technical topics.

Select the Appropriate Technical Training Methods to Promote Recall and Application

Whatever technical information is taught, it can be taught for two purposes, either to *recall* the information or to *apply* the information. The learning objective can tell you whether or not you need to train people so they merely remember something or they know how to use and apply the information. Tool 4.2 shows five types of information involved in teaching technical topics so employees can recall facts, concepts, processes, procedures, and guidelines.[1] Tool 4.3 shows how to teach technical topics so that employees can use or apply this type of information. Here are some definitions and suggested examples:

Facts are individual statements. For example: What is your password? Or which color of a five-part form goes to the customer? What is the part number for this product? What does error message 51 mean? Who is the vice president of operations? The reason you want the learner to remember this type of information/these facts is usually to do something with the information. The least effective training method is memorization. If knowing factual information is important, make sure participants practice using the facts during the training. This type of training can include "look-up" exercises or practice using job aids.

Concepts are usually stated as a classification or category or as a general idea. For example, the concept of "preferred customers" implies someone with a good credit history and deserving of special treatment. The reason you want an employee to understand the concept or remember how a concept is defined is to help the employee make a decision or to follow a policy or guideline. Thus, a "preferred" customer may receive preferred delivery, a better discount, pricing terms, etc. Train employees to recognize an example of a concept by using exercises to classify or categorize examples by matching criteria to a sample situation.

---

[1] The five types of information are based on work done by Ruth Clark (1989), *Developing Technical Training.* Reading, MA: Addison-Wesley.

Work processes and procedures are defined as steps to take and why we take them. *Process* focuses on *how* something works. *Procedures* focus on *what steps* are taken. Seventy-five percent or more of technical training involves teaching processes and procedures, for example, how to process a claim, place a telephone order, change engine oil, replace a valve, complete a repair, draw blood, or write a report. You want employees to recall or use a process or procedure so they can complete the process or procedure correctly.

On the recall level, an employee would list the steps and explain why they are taken. That's important during the training process and in high-risk situations. On the use/application level, the employee would do the steps (usually in a return demonstration). For example, during software training, it's easier to teach the content through the process. Often, by doing it (follow the steps), the learner can "discover" why it is done that way. For this type of training, first, teach the learner the steps to print a report, rather than lecture on how the report will be used and why the steps are done that way. This information can be expanded on later. Many technical processes are concerned with teaching "functionality." Can they *do* it? You don't have to know how an automobile is made to drive it safely.

Guidelines are policies, common practices, or principles that guide the use processes and procedures or the application of facts or concepts. For example, who gets credit, which customers pay before pumping their own gas, who is entitled to a refund, which part can be replaced under a warranty, which loans are funded or denied, which returned merchandise is accepted, what merchandise is shipped by surface carrier or air. The reason you want employees to be able to state criteria or guidelines is usually because they will have to explain the criteria or guidelines to customers. On the use/application level, employees must be able to apply guidelines/criteria to individual situations. The best methods to teach employees to recall and apply principles are to provide situations, case studies, or examples and ask the learners to make the decisions.

Tool 4.2. Technical Training Methods to Promote Recall[2]

	Objective Is Recall	Training Methods
Facts Unique, literal information Ex: PIN number, date, part number	Remember Identify	Job aid, online help Memorization Mnemonic cues
Concepts A classification or category of things with shared features, a mental image, a general idea, elements of a class Ex: computer, car, good credit, empathy, who is eligible for a refund	State the definition State the criteria List the guidelines	Analogies Define Give examples Demonstration Answer questions
Procedures Steps to take Ex: Put gas in a car; connect to the Internet, draw blood	List the steps Tell how to do the task	Memorize steps Tell sequence of steps
Processes Why steps are taken Ex: How to store a cell telephone number; the process for ordering office supplies, how blood circulates	Explain why steps are taken Describe how a process works	Describe Answer questions
Guidelines Policies, common practices or principles that guide the use of processes and procedures or the application of facts and concept Ex: create the next part number in a sequence	State the guideline State the criteria	Job aid Look up exercise Answer questions

[2]Special thanks to Linda Ernst, senior Training Clinic instructor, who contributed to the creation of this table.

Tool 4.3. Technical Training Methods to Promote Application

	Objective Is Use or Application	Training Method
Facts Unique, literal information Ex: PIN number, date, part number	Explain Use as part of a proce-dure, process, concept or principle	Practice
Concepts A classification or category of things with shared features, a mental image, a general idea, elements of a class, Ex: computer, car, good credit, empathy, who is eligible for a refund	Classify examples Categorize examples Apply a concept or policy Match criteria to a situation	Discrimination exercises to identify non-examples Classification activities Case studies Discussion Analogies
Procedures Steps to take Ex: Put gas in a car; connect to the Internet, draw blood	Do the steps	Sequence steps Demonstrate use Practice
Processes Why steps are taken Ex: How to store a cell telephone number; the process for ordering office supplies	Solve a problem Relate cause and effect	Practice decisions Simulations Troubleshooting exercises Read flow-charts Case studies
Guidelines Policies, common practices or principles that guide the use of processes and procedures or the application of facts and concept Ex: create the next part number in a sequence	Apply the guideline Make a decision Match criteria to a situation	Case study Role play Discrimination exercise Practice decisions

Select the Best Audiovisual Support for Materials Design and Delivery

Use the table in Tool 4.4 to identify the best audiovisual support to achieve the learning objective. "K" stands for a knowledge objective, for learning facts, theories, or visual identification. "S" stands for an objective that teaches mental or physical skill and includes analyzing or applying facts, principles, and concepts or performing a perceptual or motor skill. "A" stands for influencing attitudes, opinions, and motivations of learners. Some support media are best used to teach only one type of objective. Other media can be used effectively to teach more than one type of objective.

Tool 4.4. Select the Best Audiovisual Support[3]

Audiovisual Instructional Medium	Best Use		
	K	S	A
Audio recording	X	X	
Cartoons			X
Drawings and illustrations	X	X	
Exhibits	X		
Flip charts, whiteboards, and chalkboards	X		
Models and mock-ups	X	X	
Music			X
Overhead projection, electronic slides	X		
Photos	X		
Printed material	X	X	
Real objects	X	X	
Simulators	X	X	
Toys			X
Video, film, and TV	X	X	X

[3]Special thanks to Melissa Smith, managing partner of The Training Clinic, who helped create this chart.

Pace Training Methods to Avoid Boredom

Tool 4.5 is the Methods Variety Scale, used to vary the pace of training methods to extend the attention span of learners. The Methods Variety Scale is based on the assumption that most adults have an attention span of about 15 minutes. A recent study[4] ties attention disorders to the number of hours a preschool child watches television. If learners born after 1960 have watched an average of four or more[5] hours a day of television, could their attention span be closer to 7 minutes, since that is the programming time between commercial messages? Could learners raised in the United Kingdom watching the British Broadcasting Corporation (BBC) have an attention span closer to 20 minutes, since that is the typical length of programming? Tool 4.5 helps you capture and extend learners' attention. Here's how to read the scale.

The vertical axis shows what the learner does on a scale of 0 to 10. 0 is a low level of activity and requires little interaction with others. Most of the terms are self-evident; however, the difference between a lecture and a participative lecture is that in the latter the learners answer a few questions in the large group during a participative lecture, which increases learner involvement. A *return demonstration* is also called "practice" and usually follows a demonstration by the trainer (which is the same rating as watching a lecture or a film/video).

The horizontal axis of the Methods Variety Scale is divided into hours by solid lines and dotted lines for every 15-minute portion of time. Plot the level of learner participation during the session and check whether you have changed the pace at least every 15 minutes. Also, check to be sure that the learners' level of activity is at least over the level of 5 once an hour or more. If you do not do these two things, then learner attention and retention can still be brought higher by increasing the variety of learning activities as well as bringing the level of participation over 5 at least once an hour. For full-day workshops, try getting the level of participation over 5 at least twice an hour after lunch, when some participants would prefer to take a nap.

---

[4] Dr. Dimitri Christakis. (2004, April). Early Television Exposure and Subsequent Attentional Problems in Children. *Pediatrics, 113*(4).

[5] Wendy Josephson. (1997). *How Children Process Television*. Studio City, CA: Mediascope Press.

Many software training sessions could enhance retention by using this scale. In particular, the developers limit themselves to demonstration (level 2) and a return demonstration (level 9). During software training, you can improve on this by using learner practice followed by two or three return demonstrations. Many software training sessions use only the first two steps in the five steps of the adult learning model. Try having a large or small group instruction for the learners to share and interpret their reactions to what they have been practicing. Then ask them the concept they have discovered while practicing with the software, and finally, ask them how they can apply what they have learned in their own work. Breaking up practice sessions by using a variety of methods can avoid overloading participants with too much information in a compressed period of time.

Use Tool 4.5 to check the pace of learning activities so attention and retention can improve.

Tool 4.5. Methods Variety Scale[6]

Instructions: Plot learners' level of participation. Vary classroom learners' activity at least every 15 minutes. Vary online learners' activity at least every 2 minutes for a webinar, every 5 minutes for virtual instructor-led training. Raise learners' participation over the level of 5 at least once an hour before lunch, twice an hour after lunch.

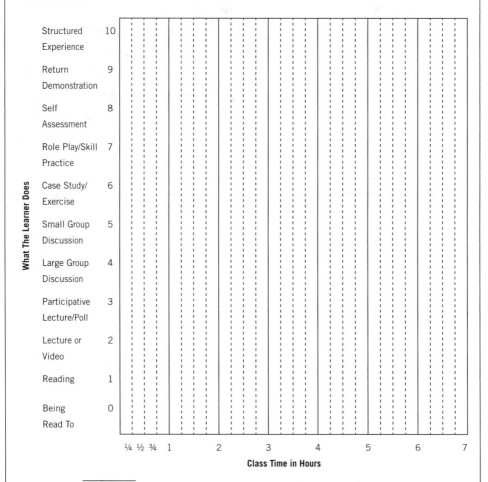

[6]© 1986. The Training Clinic, *The Art of Great Training Delivery*, 2nd edition. Copyright © 2006 by Jean Barbazette. Reproduced by permission of Pfeiffer, an Imprint of Wiley. www.pfeiffer.com

Determine How Much Practice Is Needed to Learn a New Skill[7]

The purpose of the decision tree analysis in Tool 4.6 is for you to decide how much training and practice is appropriate for participants to learn a new task, based on the task's difficulty, importance, and frequency with which the task will be regularly done.

Of course, it is more *difficult* to learn how to do a task than to do a task once learned. "Difficulty" in this context refers to once the task is learned, not the difficulty of learning it. Some factors that make a task difficult to do once it is learned include complexity, the number of steps in a task, the requirement to complete steps in a specific sequence, degree of physical dexterity needed, the requirement for uniform performance of the task, environmental factors, degree of physical or professional risk, and the length of time to complete the task. Also consider the difficulty for the typical performer Assess the level of difficulty of learning the task from one learner's point of view. Remember also that an individual's attitude toward doing the task successfully can make the task seem harder.

Tasks have relative *importance* to managers, supervisors, and employees. Perceived importance and organizational importance of doing a task in a standard manner are both worth considering. To what degree will the task outcome change based on irregular performance? Are there consequences for poor performance? Ask whether or not it is important to do this task in a prescribed, standard manner.

Will the task be repeated *frequently* enough so the employee will not forget how to do the task once learned, or is lots of practice necessary to build initial and permanent retention?

Once you have identified the *difficulty, importance,* and *frequency* of a task, use Tool 4.6 to decide how much training is usually sufficient to learn and retain a task and the type of reinforcement that is appropriate. A few examples are given below, with a rationale for each recommendation.

---

[7]Based on a tool from the Army School of Instructional Technology, UK Royal Army Education Corps, Pamphlet No. 2, "Job Analysis for Training," Army Code No. 70670.

If a participant is to learn to do cardiopulmonary resuscitation (CPR), the task is very difficult, since CPR is performed during life-and-death circumstances, and it is physically demanding to do for more than a few minutes. CPR must be performed in a standardized manner and is infrequently performed by even healthcare practitioners in hospital emergency rooms. The recommendation is to provide *advanced training,* which means that learners must be trained to a high standard of retention, accomplished by reinforcement training, resources, references, or job aids. This explains why CPR certification must be renewed annually and why learners are given a job aid to carry with them as a reminder of the process learned in class.

An example of a task learned by most new employees during orientation to a new job is to complete a time card or account for their hours worked on a daily or weekly basis. Most systems (punch cards, software programs) are not difficult to complete. It is important to complete the task in a standardized way, since most systems only accept data in a predetermined manner. This task will be completed very frequently (daily or weekly). The recommendation is to use demonstration because formal training is not required, and the skill can be acquired on the job through practice. There is also the added motivation to report hours correctly to receive one's paycheck on time.

A final example is to create a script or lesson plan from a PowerPoint presentation. For many people, it is a moderately difficult task to perform. This task includes modifying the slides after they are imported into a Word document. To correctly export the slides, a standardized process is followed. If the learners will use this feature of PowerPoint frequently, basic training is recommended. That will ensure that the learners can demonstrate proficiency in performing this task at an achievement level required on the job. Notice that if this task is to be only moderately or infrequently performed, advanced training is recommended. That may mean providing a job aid as a reminder of the steps in this process.

Tool 4.6. DIF: How Much Practice and Training?

How difficult is the task to do?	Important that task be done in standardized manner?		How frequently will task be repeated?	Recommendation
Very ⇒	Important that task be done in standardized manner?	Yes ⇒	How frequently will task be repeated?	Very ⇒ **Basic** Moderate ⇒ **Advanced** Infrequent ⇒ **Advanced**
		No ⇒	How frequently will task be repeated?	Very ⇒ **Basic** Moderate ⇒ **Basic** Infrequent ⇒ **Demonstrate**
Moderate ⇒	Important that task be done in standardized manner?	Yes ⇒	How frequently will task be repeated?	Very ⇒ **Basic** Moderate ⇒ **Advanced** Infrequent ⇒ **Advanced**
		No ⇒	How frequently will task be repeated?	Very ⇒ **Demonstrate** Moderate ⇒ **Demonstrate** Infrequent ⇒ **Demonstrate**
Not ⇒	Important that task be done in standardized manner?	Yes ⇒	How frequently will task be repeated?	Very ⇒ **Demonstrate** Moderate ⇒ **Demonstrate** Infrequent ⇒ **Demonstrate**
		No ⇒	How frequently will task be repeated?	Very ⇒ **Demonstrate** Moderate ⇒ **Demonstrate** Infrequent ⇒ **Demonstrate**

DIF Practice Recommendation

Difficulty—Importance—Frequency

- *Demonstrate:* Formal training not required. Skills can be acquired on the job through practice after a demonstration.

- *Basic Training:* Learner must be able to demonstrate proficiency in performing task at achievement level required on the job.

- *Advanced Training:* Learner must be trained to a high standard of retention. Accomplished by reinforcement training, resources, references, or job aids.

How to Write Terrific Training Materials. Copyright © 2013 by John Wiley & Sons, Inc. Reproduced by permission of Pfeiffer, an Imprint of Wiley, www.pfeiffer.com.

Sequence Training Methods Using a Situational Training Model

The next step in writing training materials is to decide how to sequence training methods. Sequencing training steps or methods depends on the learning objective and three factors to be assessed about the learners: experience, education, and motivation. Look at Tool 4.7 for guidance in deciding how to sequence training steps and methods.

Style 1 is called "demonstrate." The sequence of training methods is to tell the learners what they are going to see, show them the process, and supervise or guide practice in a return demonstration. Style 1 is teaching a skill, and your assessment of the learners' maturity is low.

Style 2 is called "lecture/test." The sequence of training methods is to tell the learners new information, ask them for feedback so they can tell the trainer what they have understood, and conduct an exercise or case study to help the learners apply new information. Style 2 is used to teach new information, and your assessment of the learners' maturity is low.

Style 3 is called "learning experience." The sequence of training methods is to begin with an activity or learning experience, ask the learners to share and interpret their reactions to the activity, generalize concepts from what they have experienced, and apply new concepts to the job. Style 3 is used to teach new skills, and your assessment of the learners' maturity is high.

Style 4 is called "case study." The sequence of training methods is to begin with a case study, simulation, game, or experience. Next learners are asked to share and interpret their reactions to the case study, generalize concepts from the case study, and apply new concepts to what they now know about their jobs. Style 4 is used to teach new information, and your assessment of the learners' maturity is high.

Notice that Styles 1 and 3 have learning objectives that teach a new skill. Styles 2 and 4 have learning objectives that teach new information. Notice that Styles 1 and 2 are very instructor-directed and Styles 3 and 4 are learner-directed.

One of the benefits of this model is that the course developer can refer back to the target population analysis to determine the maturity (experience, education, and motivation) of the learners. If the target population changes, the instructor can re-sequence the order of the training methods. For example, if the learners are being taught to ask appropriate (legal) questions during a selection interview, a manager who has conducted selection interviews for many years might be insulted or diminished by being told (Style 2) what questions to ask. If a manager has many years of experience, or the self-perception of many years of experience, begin with a case study and ask the manager to identify which questions are appropriate or in appropriate and why.

Tool 4.7. Situational Training Methods Model

Facilitator Style

	Instructor-Directed	**Learner-Directed**
Do/Skill	**Demonstrate** Style 1 1. Tell 2. Show 3. Guided practice *(Instructor-Directed)*	**Learning Experience** Style 3 1. Learning experience/ activity 2. Share and interpret reactions 3. Generalize concepts from the experience 4. Apply concepts to new experiences *(Learner-Directed)*
Know/ Understand	**Lecture/Test** Style 2 1. Tell them 2. They tell you what they know 3. Exercise/case study to apply new information *(Instructor-Directed)*	**Case Study** Style 4 1. Case study, simulation, game, or experience 2. Share and interpret reactions 3. Generalize concepts from the experience 4. Apply concepts to new experiences *(Learner-Directed)*

(Objective — vertical axis label)

| **Low** | **High** |

Learner Assessment

- Experience
- Education
- Motivation

Describe How the Materials Development Process Changes Based on Classroom Versus e-Learning Delivery

How does the process of writing training materials differ when the delivery medium is e-learning? First, there are some considerations for lack of face-to-face delivery. First-time learners appreciate an orientation to e-learning and the virtual classroom. Here are some suggestions to include in a lesson plan for virtual delivery:

Write a confirmation letter:

1. Tell how to do a system check the day before class.

2. Connect to synchronous events 15 to 30 minutes before the start of the session.

3. Be sure to provide the user sign-in and password for the event. Provide a method to remind those who forget or misplace sign-in information.

Write directions to greet participants when they enter the virtual classroom:

1. Have the administrator introduce him- or herself and tell the role of the administrator, who will monitor chat, troubleshoot technical problems, etc.

2. Do a sound check and tell participants how to adjust sound volume from their desktops.

Write directions to acquaint the learner with platform tools:

1. Write a description of a virtual tour of the tools by demonstrating each tool through an activity.

2. Write polling questions.

3. Ask several easy-to-answer questions to help the group to interact and use the chat feature, whiteboard, and drawing tools.

Write directions for off-air assignments:

1. Provide written directions for posting comments, posting content (blogging), and asking questions in email.

2. Give time frames and deadlines for assignments.

3. Write guidelines for when to write a blog or a question (something of interest to all or typical questions) and when to send email to the instructor (private concerns).

Exhibit 4.2 lists of tools necessary for online learning. Exhibit 4.2 shows some additional materials that need to be written for virtual courses. They include administrative information as well as course materials. Exhibit 4.3 offers suggestions the course developer can share with the virtual facilitator about how to connect with the virtual learner on several occasions. Finally, Exhibit 4.4 offers suggestions to pass along to virtual instructors to compensate for the lack of face-to-face contact.

Next Steps

The next chapter will help you develop/write training materials suggested in this chapter.

Exhibit 4.1. Tools to Promote Interaction

Synchronous Learning Tools

Whiteboards for brainstorming and drawing

Polling

Testing

Asking questions

Subgrouping with a specific assignment

Application sharing

Virtual tours

Streaming media

Participant evaluation form

Asynchronous Learning Tools

Off-air assignments that require research, reading, and posting

Threaded discussions

Email

Polling

Asking questions

Testing

Participant evaluation forms

Internet searches

Exhibit 4.2. Materials and Other Logistics

As part of a script or lesson plan, create a list of all the information and materials you need for a course:

Administrative Information

- Class roster with email contact information
- Copy of confirmation of enrollment sent to participants
- Sign-on and password information
- How to get technical support
- How to find course materials
- How and where to send email assignments
- Posting assignments, where and how to post
- Grading system

Course Materials

- Written handout materials, including text books and bibliography
- Visuals
- Polling questions
- Written questions or other activities to increase interaction and participation
- Off-air assignments

Exhibit 4.3. Connect with the Virtual Learner

There are several opportunities to connect with the virtual learner. To build a virtual community takes work and continual effort over a period of time.

Before the course begins

Following enrollment of a participant into your course, send a confirmation email to each participant. Thank him or her for enrolling, tell about pre-course assignments and some of your expectations for the course. Provide resources for questions and technical assistance.

Post a picture of yourself along with a brief introduction. Ask learners to introduce themselves.

During the course

Ask questions and use interaction and participation techniques described in later chapters.

Explain course objectives, assignments, and your grading system.

Give individual feedback to postings. If a participant has a long post, copy the few sentences that describe the main point and ask a question to help the participants to think in greater depth about the topic.

Make a general posting that clarifies previous points or redirects the group.

Give individual feedback for off-air assignments. If you subgroup participants for off-air assignments, give group feedback about the quality, substance, and originality of the assignment.

Offer suggestions for additional reading or resources on a specific topic, especially if the topic would take you off-course.

Set a specific time for group email when participants can expect an answer within an hour of sending their emails.

Encourage preparation for tests by offering study questions or material that needs review.

Give participants feedback on tests.

At the conclusion of the course

Congratulate participants and award certificates of completion.

Exhibit 4.4. Compensate for Lack of Face-to-Face Contact

- Ask participants to post electronic pictures of themselves with an introduction.
- Rehearse synchronous events and obtain feedback from a pilot group.
- Give extra preparation when writing questions to gain interaction. Be sure the question is asked appropriately to obtain the type of answer you intend.
- Use participants' names when asking questions, giving feedback, or responding to posts and assignments.
- Place pins or flags on a map to show where participants live.
- Ask participants for local news.
- Use descriptive words to paint a picture.
- Get a book/article on visualization and learn more about how to create mental images.

Develop Materials for Learning Activities

This chapter will help the developer to:

- Write three types of materials, depending on the purpose
- Use a seven-step process to design learning activities
- Adapt and modify existing activities
- Create discovery learning by writing five adult learning steps to process any learning activity
- Distinguish the use of different types of handout materials
- Edit materials to address content and format issues
- Develop effective and lean job aids
- Use different graphic looks to enhance training materials

Tools

- 5.1. Seven-Step Process to Design Learning Materials
- 5.2. Adapt or Modify Existing Materials
- 5.3. Content and Format Summary

- 5.4. Job Aid Development
- 5.5. Job Aid Formats

Exhibits

- 5.1. Branded and Non-Branded Documents
- 5.2. Emotional Graphics
- 5.3. Systems and Non-Systems Graphic Sets
- 5.4. Sample Icon Sets
- 5.5. Negative Example and Well-Placed Example

Write Three Types of Materials, Depending on the Purpose

There are three reasons someone will read the materials you develop:

1. Some will read to gain knowledge or improve their understanding of an idea.

2. Some will read to be able to do something they currently don't know how to do.

3. Some will read to reflect and integrate new ideas with their current mind sets.

The materials developer must keep in mind the reader's purpose when writing for each purpose. If the reader wants to learn something, write to *inform* so the reader can gain new information and knowledge and is able to improve an understanding of an idea. If the reader wants to do something he or she can't currently do, write to *direct* the reader by describing specific steps. If the reader wants to reflect on ideas, write materials to *persuade* the reader. Here are two examples that show three different purposes for writing materials on the same topic:

Example 1: Changing a tire on a car (initial steps)

Purpose: read to learn (write to inform or impart knowledge):

"For safety sake, when changing the tire on a car, stay out of the way of other traffic. The gearshift should be set in park and the hand brake set."

Purpose: read to do (write to direct):

"When changing a tire on a car, follow these steps:

* Park the car away from the flow of traffic.
* Set the gearshift in park.
* Set the hand brake in park."

Purpose: read to reflect (write to persuade):

"Think safety and convenience. Let our roadside assistance technician change your tire for you."

Example 2: Withdrawing/depositing money from an ATM

Purpose: read to learn (write to inform or impart knowledge):

"Automatic tellers are a great convenience and so easy to use. They may not be friendly or smile, but they are always ready to serve you with efficiency. Deposits and withdrawals are made using an encoded plastic card."

Purpose: read to do (write to direct):

"To make a withdrawal or a deposit using an automatic teller machine, follow these steps:

- Place card right side up in the card slot.
- Enter personal identification code number.
- Identify the account for the transaction.
- For a deposit, enter the amount being deposited.
- Place check or cash in slot.
- Remove card and receipt."

Purpose: read to reflect (write to persuade):

"Collect customer rewards. Use the ATM for all of your banking needs."

Use a Seven-Step Process to Design Learning Activities

Once you have identified the purpose the reader has in mind for reading materials you are about to develop, follow this seven-step process to be sure you have developed materials for the best learning experience and retention.

1. Identify the business need to develop specific training materials: What bottom-line results will occur from a learner completing this class? Will sales increase; will accidents decrease; will work be completed more efficiently? Begin to build a partnership with the manager of those who will attend the training session.

2. Identify the class: What is the primary focus of the program? What is the time limit of the class, if any?

3. Identify the target population: Who will be attending the program? How many at a time? Will different levels attend the class at the same time? (For additional information on how to conduct a Target Population Analysis, see *Training Needs Assessment,* Chapter 8.)

4. Write the learning objective: What do you want the learner to be able to do by the end of the session?

    To accomplish this, will you:

    • Give information, inform, or develop a new understanding?

    • Teach skills, change behaviors, or practice skills?

    • Influence attitudes, opinions, or feelings?

    Is your objective a combination of these three types of objectives?

5. Decide *how* you will evaluate whether learning objectives are reached. You don't need to create a test or skill practice at this point of development; rather, just decide how you will measure the learning objectives.

6. Choose the delivery medium (classroom training, online learning, blended mediums, etc.). (To learn more about selecting the appropriate delivery medium, consult Contextual Analysis in *Training Needs Assessment,* Chapter 9.)

7. Develop learner materials by adapting or modifying existing content or creating the content, including visual aids.

    • Select the best learning experience(s) to meet the instructional objective (see Tool 4.1).

- Write instructions and questions for the five steps of adult learning to process the learning activity.

1. Set up the learning activity.
2. Complete the learning activity.
3. Learners share and interpret their reactions to the activity.
4. Learners identify concepts from their reactions.
5. Learners apply concepts to their situations.

- Decide how much practice is required to learn this material (see Tool 4.6).
- Pace the learner's activity level to avoid boredom (see Tool 4.5).
- Determine what type of knowledge or skill test (activity) will be used to identify to what extent the learning objective has been met.
- Develop a leader's guide (see Chapter 11).

These seven steps are the blueprint to develop training materials. A template that summarizes the seven-step process is shown in Tool 5.1. Next, check whether you have existing materials that you can use or adapt, or whether you need to write new materials.

Tool 5.1. Seven-Step Process to Design Learning Materials

1. Identify the business need to develop specific training materials. Begin to build a partnership with the manager of those who will attend the training session.

2. Identify the class: What is the primary focus of the program? What is the time limit of the class, if any?

3. Identify the target population: Who will be attending the program? How many at a time? Will different levels attend the class at the same time?

4. Write the learning objective: What do you want the learner to be able to do by the end of the session?

   • Give information, inform, or develop a new understanding?

   • Teach skills, change behaviors, or practice skills?

   • Influence attitudes, opinions, or feelings?

   Is your objective a combination of these three types of objectives?

5. Decide *how* you will evaluate whether learning objectives are reached.

6. Choose the delivery medium (classroom training, online learning, blended mediums, etc.).

7. Develop learner materials by adapting or modifying existing content or creating the content, including visual aids.

   • Select the best learning experience(s) to meet the instructional objective.

   • Write instructions and questions for the five steps of adult learning to process the learning activity.

Tool 5.1. Seven-Step Process to Design Learning Materials *(continued)*

1. Set up the learning activity.

2. Complete the learning activity.

3. Learners share and interpret their reactions to the activity.

4. Learners identify concepts from their reactions.

5. Learners apply concepts to their situations.

- Use DIF analysis to identify how much practice is required to learn this material.

- Use the Methods Variety Scale to pace the learner's activity level to avoid boredom

- Write a knowledge or skill test (activity) to identify to what extent the learning objective has been met.

- Develop a leader's guide.

Adapt, Modify or Create New Learning Experiences

Ask these key questions to decide whether to adapt or modify existing materials or create new materials:

- Do materials of the type you want to use already exist within your organization? If so, acquire and use them with the permission of the materials owner.

- Are appropriate materials available from an external source? Is it easier and more cost-effective to acquire these than use alternative methods or produce your own materials? If you are buying software from an external vendor, ask what training materials exist to help users work with the software.

- Would alternative materials serve your purpose equally well? Sometimes materials have been developed for another purpose. For example, if the marketing department has product knowledge materials, could those materials be repurposed for new employee orientation or to train internal repair technicians?

- Can you modify an activity to reach your learning objective? (See *Instant Case Studies* (Barbazette, 2004) for seventy case studies that can be customized.)

- Is it practical to produce your own materials? Do you have the time and skill to develop new materials?

Be sure to obtain copyright permission to use materials developed/owned by someone else.

If none of the questions in Tool 5.1 produce satisfactory answers, consider alternative methods of achieving your instructional objectives and start again, or begin to create new materials. Before leaving the topic of adapting or modifying training materials, look at Tool 5.2 for practical steps to slightly alter existing materials for a new purpose or audience.

Tool 5.2. Adapt or Modify Existing Materials

Write a statement that identifies the purpose of the current materials. For example, *the product descriptions will help sales representatives match the appropriate product to the right customer.* Next, write a new purpose statement for a different use of the same materials. For example, *the product descriptions will help the new employee identify the wide range of products available from our company.* Comparing these two statements will help you decide how to repurpose learner materials.

1. Write a learning objective for the learner. For example, *given product descriptions and a storage map, the new shipping clerk will identify where to find each product in our warehouse.*

2. Decide whether the objective is intended to teach knowledge, develop skill, or influence the employee's attitude. In the example above, the new employee will develop knowledge about storage locations for different products.

3. Review the Best Learning Experiences chart (Tool 4.1) and identify what method(s) will reach the knowledge objective. For this example, information search, learning tournament, printed resources, and study groups could all be used to reach this objective.

4. Write instructions and processing questions to set up the learning activity and debrief it using the five steps of adult learning. (The five steps are explained in more detail later in this chapter.)

5. After selecting the products to identify, use DIF analysis (Tool 4.6) to identify how much practice is required to learn this new material. In our example, how many products or groups of products will the new shipping clerk locate in order to demonstrate an understanding of how products are organized in the warehouse?

6. Use the Methods Variety Scale (Tool 4.5) to be sure the learner's level of activity is varied every 15 minutes, and reaches the level of five or more each hour. In our example, the new shipping clerks can work in pairs and share their results after a 15-minute search.

7. Develop a knowledge or skill test. In the example, the facilitator can determine whether the shipping clerks have found the product in the correct location. The activity actually becomes the "test." (More information about writing tests is in Chapter 10.)

8. Develop the leader's guide. (Chapter 11 describes three types of leader's guides and how to write each one.)

9. After determining whether you will adapt or modify existing materials or design new materials, consider how to direct the trainer or facilitator to process learning activities to gain the most from any learning experience. The five-step adult learning model is recommended.

Create Discovery Learning by Developing Five Adult Learning Steps to Process Any Learning Activity

How can adults get the most from any learning experience? Use a discovery learning process. When you *tell* learners new information, it doesn't belong to them. If learners *discover* a new concept, it belongs to them. To create discovery learning, use the five step adult learning process explained below.

Many trainers are familiar with an experiential learning model that takes learners through a series of steps to process a learning activity such as a simulation. This type of activity and debriefing discussion is helpful and appropriate for any type of learning activity. Here is a general description of what takes place during the five steps of adult learning.[1] The successful trainer or facilitator guides adult learners through these five steps to gain the most from any learning activity. These five steps are similar to many experiential learning models.

1. Trainer Sets Up the Learning Activity by Telling What, Why, and How

Set up the learning activity so the participants understand *what* they are going to do (for example, read a case study and individually prepare answers for a discussion) and *why* they are doing it (learn about how to give a performance review). Adult learners become motivated when they understand the benefit to them of learning something new or the importance of an objective for themselves. To understand *how* the objective will be met, give directions and ground rules regarding how the learning activity is to be conducted. The set-up of a learning activity can include such things as:

- Tell participants the purpose of the learning activity and why they are going to learn from the activity without giving away what is to be "discovered."

- Explain what the participants are going to do.

- Review the written directions and answer questions about the activity.

---

[1] Adapted from Jean Barbazette. (2001). *Instant Case Studies.* San Francisco: Pfeiffer. Used with permission.

- Divide participants into small groups or explain the amount of time to prepare individually for a group activity.

- Assign small group roles such as recorder, reporter, or small group discussion leader.

- Give other ground rules.

2. Learners Participate in a Learning Activity

For a learning activity to be successful, involve learners as much as possible. Consider how learning from a specific activity will appeal to different learning styles. This step might include individual reading of a case study, reading background information for a simulation, or other preparation, such as following the written directions given at the beginning of the activity, reading questions to be answered as the class watches a video, following the learners' discussion, or asking a reporter from each small group to share that group's answers.

3. Learners Share and Interpret Their Reactions

This step is essential to help conclude the small group discussions and gives learners the opportunity to identify what happened in different small groups. Ask the group additional questions to help learners analyze the discussion and then develop individual and group reactions to the activity. Have learners share their reactions by identifying what happened to them and to others and how their behavior affected others during the small group discussion. Sample facilitator processing questions are

- "What made it easy or difficult to find a solution to this problem?"
- "What helped or hindered the progress of the discussion?"
- "Let's summarize the key points from the case study."

Sometimes, it is appropriate to have participants write down their reactions so that others do not influence their thinking before they share reactions to a learning activity. In this way, the reactions come from the learners, not from the facilitator.

Sharing reactions is the beginning step of reaching a conclusion. If participants do not take this step, it is difficult to end the activity and move on, as there may be unfinished business that spills over into later activities. Some learners have difficulty moving on without the "right" answer.

4. Learners Identify Concepts

This is the "So what did I learn from the activity?" step. If this step is left out, then learning will be incomplete. Up to this point, participants have been actively learning from a specific situation and may not be able to generalize their learning to similar situations outside the classroom. Questions that help learners develop concepts include:

- "What did you learn about how to conduct an interview, discipline a subordinate, teach a new job, etc., from this learning activity?"

- "What is appropriate behavior for a new supervisor?"

- "What does the successful salesperson do to close the sale?"

When concepts are fleshed out from a discussion of the learning activity, adult learners are ready to apply these concepts to future situations. Ask questions to elicit concepts from the learners, rather than tell them the concepts they should have found.

5. Learners Apply Concepts to Their Own Situations

This is the "So what now?" step in the adult learning process. Ask participants how they can use and apply the new information they have learned. Ask questions like:

- "How will you use this skill the next time a subordinate asks you for a favor?"

- "What are some situations in which you would be more effective if you used this technique?"

If this step is left out, learners may not see the relationship between the learning activity and their own jobs or situations. This step stresses practical application and helps learners find the personal benefits from the learning activity.

To effectively facilitate a discussion of any learning activity, ask the learners questions about the learning activity, rather than suggesting applications. When learners discover the concept, they are more likely to apply it to their own situation. Following are Facilitator Processing Questions[2] to elicit discovery learning using Steps 3, 4, and 5.

Questions for Step 3: Learners Share and Interpret Their Reactions

- What happened when you tried out that function/step as part of the activity?
- What surprised you?
- What part was easy? Difficult? What made it easy? Difficult?
- What did you notice/observe? How was that significant?
- How was that positive/negative?
- What struck you most about that?
- How do these pieces fit together?

Questions for Step 4: Learners Identify Concepts

- How does this relate to other parts of the process?
- What might we conclude from that?
- What did you learn/relearn?
- What processes/steps are similar to this one?
- What else is this step/process like?
- What does that suggest to you about _____ in general?
- What's important to remember about this step/function?
- What other options/ways do you have for completing this step/function?
- How can you integrate this step into the larger process?
- What other functions are impacted by this step?

---

[2]Adapted from J. William Pfeiffer. (1988). *UA Training Technologies 7: Presentation and Evaluation Skills in Human Resource Development* (pp. 66–68). San Francisco: Pfeiffer. Used with permission.

Questions for Step 5: Learners Apply Concepts to Their Own Situations

- How can you use what you have learned?

- What is the value of this step/function?

- What would be the consequence of doing/not doing the step?

- How does what you have learned fit with your experience?

After considering how to process an adult learning activity using the five steps above, next consider what type of learner handout materials will promote learning and retention.

Distinguish the Use of Different Types of Handout Materials

There are five different types of learner handout materials:

1. *Pre-work materials* are given to the learners prior to attending the training session. They are intended to prepare the learners, create some interest in the topic, and save valuable class time for higher levels of learning activities.

2. *Programmed notes* are an outline of topics to be covered during the training.

3. *Exercises, case studies,* and *learning activities* are described extensively in Chapters 6, 7, 8, and 9.

4. *Tests* are described in Chapter 10.

5. *Reference materials and job aids* are provided as resource material and not intended to be covered during class time.

Pre-Work

Types of pre-work assignments include:

- *Reading.* Send copies of textbooks, articles, or materials to read prior to the training program. Materials are most effective if sent along with discussion questions. Giving a pretest to identify what was learned from the reading materials increases the probability that the materials will be read.

- *Complete an assignment.* Send an exercise or have participants complete an activity that can be a benchmark for performance that is refined during the workshop. For example, participants can survey co-workers on a topic that will be covered during the workshop.

- *Gather and bring.* Have participant identify and bring a work sample or work product that will be used during the workshop. For example, participants can be asked to identify a topic for a sample presentation. Or participants can gather department statistics, last year's budget figures, etc., in preparation for an activity that will use those figures.

- *Complete and return.* Ask participants to complete a survey prior to the workshop that identifies their skill level, inventories their interest or expectations, or offers their opinions on topics to be addressed during the workshop.

Programmed Notes

Programmed notes give essential information to the learner in an outline form. This has two benefits: (1) the learner does not need to write down everything that the instructor says and (2) the learner can write down what he or she wants to remember. Some learners write definitions, examples, applications, or nothing at all. Note-taking often depends on the learner's preferred style to take in and process information.

Some instructors or course developers provide a copy of PowerPoint slides for note-taking.

Edit Materials to Address Content and Format Issues

Chapter 3 suggested three types of editing: big picture revision, what's the point revision, and detail revision. Big picture revision includes possible format changes. Tool 5.3 provides points to consider when editing handout format. What's the point revision is proving that the message is clear, concise, and simply presented. Handout content editing points also appear in Tool 5.3.

Tool 5.3. Content and Format Summary

Developing effective handout materials involves two types of issues: *content* and *format*.

Handout Format

- Varied prose and outline form

- Enough white space

- Enough writing space

- Consistent graphic "look"—use of icons

- Well organized: numbered pages, section dividers, table of contents, index

- Title to identify the page immediately

- Appropriate binding

Handout Content

- Clean and clear

- Concise, to the point

- Enough examples to reinforce and/or make the point

- Allows for practice or exercises

- Follows logical sequence

- Accurate information

- Grammatically correct

- Further references (where to go for more information or help)

Develop Effective and Lean Job Aids[3]

Job aids are a type of handout material intended as a quick reference tool to be used back on the job. Tool 5.4 shows a six-step process to develop job aids. It is also an example of a job aid.

There are six formats to develop job aids. To help you decide which format to use, review the examples in Tool 5.5. The six types of job aid formats and their purposes are

1. *Cookbook:* a sequential list of task steps

2. *Worksheet:* a sequential list of task steps that require some explanation

3. *Decision table:* a series of "if-then" options

4. *Flowchart:* a presentation of a series of decisions

5. *Checklist:* a review-oriented list

6. *Information list:* a tool for presenting a lot of essential information

---

[3]Adapted from Allison Rossett and Jeannette Gautier-Downes (1991). *A Handbook of Job Aids.* San Francisco: Pfeiffer. Used with permission.

Tool 5.4. Job Aid Development

1	Clarify the issue to be addressed by the job aid.	What is the best way of doing or approaching the task? Write down each step in detail. What are the common errors or misjudgments made by users? What kinds and level of help is needed by the user?
2	Choose the format and medium.	Who will be using the job aid? What is the working environment? What job aid development resources are available? What part of the task is being supported by the job aid? Consider the user's background, level of experience with the task, and previous experience with documentation.
3	Prepare a draft of the job aid.	Concentrate on "how" in the job aid's title or on what exactly the aid does for users. Stick to a consistent template or style. Allow for white space so the user can add notes. Limit the job aid to one page or two pages back-to-back. Place a creation/revision date and page numbers in the footer of the document. Provide examples when appropriate. Lead with action verbs and highlight those verbs. Emphasize action, but do not ignore "why." Present information in small bits. Use tables, graphics, bulleted lists, and drawings. Proofread your document.
4	Pilot the job aid.	Ask end-users to complete the task using the job aid. Observe the performance and ask about use of the job aid.
5	Make revisions to the job aid.	Make revisions based on feedback and pilot test. Get a final sign-off from subject-matter experts and management. Place a creation/revision date and page numbers in the footer of the document. Reproduce and distribute the job aid. If appropriate, add to relevant training programs.
6	Manage the job aid.	Supply more than enough for every employee and work area. Determine how and when revisions will be initiated and who will initiate the revisions and remove outdated versions.

Tool 5.5. Job Aid Formats

Cookbook: Use for a sequential list of task steps. Think of a recipe!

- Begin with the name of the task.

- List the steps or procedures in sequential order.

- Number all steps or procedures.

- Make sure that steps are small enough to recall and perform successfully.

- Use precise language

- Use simple graphics, if appropriate.

Task: Fill out form	
#	Procedure
1	Enter applicant's name on line 1.
2	Enter temporary address on line 2.

Worksheet: Use for a sequential list of steps that require some instruction.

Tips. . .

- Use the name of the task in the worksheet title.

- Present directions before the response is entered.

- Provide sufficient space for responses.

Worksheet for Calculating Income

Week	Enter Hours	Hourly Rate	Hrs. X Rate
1		$20	
2		$20	
3		$20	
4		$20	
		Add weekly totals:	

Tool 5.5. Job Aid Formats *(continued)*

Decision Table: Use for presenting decision alternatives.

Tips. . .

- Make sure that all critical "if" statements are listed.

- Check that the "then" statement fully addresses the situation in the "if" statement.

- Arrange the statement in order with the most frequently occurring situation listed first.

If Customer. . .	Then. . .
Asks about eligibility requirements.	Instruct them to call the toll-free customer service number.

Flow Chart: Use for presenting decision alternatives.

Tips. . .

- State all items as questions.

- Give immediate yes/no options following each question.

- Present the most common situation first (the one that will reduce the number of users who will need to read through the entire chart).

- Use simple questions that have limited answers.

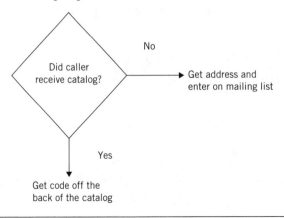

Checklist: Use for review-oriented tasks.

Tips. . .

- List the name of the task first.

- Leave space for the name of the checklist users and other relevant data (date, time, conditions, etc.).

- Provide room for notes or comments.

- Cluster and label related items for ease of completion.

- Sequence the items in a logical flow.

- Use precise language.

Task: Review job aids

Items	Notes
No editorial errors	
Job aid type is appropriate	
Items sequenced properly	
Content matter is accurate	

Information List: Use for presenting lots of data. Answers who, what, or where.

Tips. . .

- Describe the information/data first.

- Organize the data in a logical format with obvious meaning.

- List the specific version of data that the job aid fits.

Change Codes	
C01	Incorrect account number
C02	Incorrect transit routing number
C03	Account name change
C04	Incorrect transaction code

Use Different Graphic Looks to Enhance Training Materials

First Impressions: Make Your Materials Shine[4]

Like it or not, your learners will judge a training event by how the materials look. Did you use sporadic clip art on handouts? Are the workbooks full of dense text? Are the pages numbered? Do the job aids look like something a seventh-grade teacher photocopied a dozen times before handing out? All of these "shortcuts" speak volumes about the training. And the message isn't good.

There are a handful of best practices to designing polished, professional, and wow-inspiring materials. The benefit isn't just aesthetic, either. Well-designed materials support the learning experience and knowledge transfer process. After you have determined what types of materials you need (using the other tools in this chapter), follow the steps below to make sure your materials make a great impression.

Know your branding: Whether you are creating materials for a privately held financial firm, a government agency, or a non-profit, every organization has a brand. It doesn't matter whether you are an internal practitioner or an external consultant, you should make sure to utilize the company's logo and colors on all materials. If there isn't an established color palette, create one using the colors of the company's logo and choosing colors that are complementary to it. Include at least one color as an accent; this should be only used to emphasize content. Limit the colors to no more than five.

Exhibit 5.1 is an example of a "branded" and "non-branded" worksheet:

---

[4]Contributed by Jenn Labin and Insoo Kim. Used with permission.

Exhibit 5.1. Branded and Non-Branded Documents

A Branded Document

This document contains consistent fonts, colors as well as imagery. If a learner were to compare this document to other materials in the same class, they would easily be able to recognize the similarities in style.

Page 1

A Non-Branded Document

This document is inconsistent and uses too many fonts. The logo is not formatted properly. It is does not look the same as other materials and therefore does not appear professional.

PAGE 1

Develop a concept: It will be your driving force in choosing images, colors, and other graphics. The topic of your workshop will help develop the concept. Why is there a need for the workshop? What is the ultimate goal? What will your audience receive from the material?

Choose a mood: Spend a few minutes to figure out the impact you want to make with your materials. Is this a workshop on time management? You probably want to keep things conservative and minimalist. What about a class on innovation or a new sales line? Try pushing the envelope a little bit with bright colors (within your branding!) and big graphics. Exhibit 5.2 shows examples of "emotional" graphics.

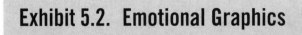

Exhibit 5.2. Emotional Graphics

Decide on an image system: Most people write content and then at the last minute throw some stock images onto the page. You want to make sure you choose a *system* of images. That means that all of the images look like they belong together. Are you going to predominately use photographs or digitally created images (graphics created on the computer rather than taken by a camera)? If you choose photos, are you going to use black and white or color? An easy way to make different images look similar is by adding a color background or frame to each one. Exhibit 5.3 shows image collages of graphics or photos that might be on materials. Can you tell the difference between the "systems" and "non-systems"?

Exhibit 5.3. Systems and Non-Systems Graphic Sets

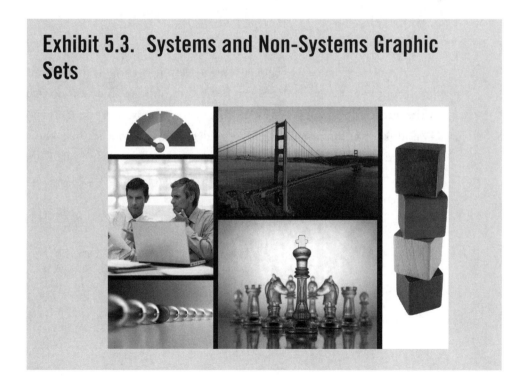

Use icons: A great way to help encourage learning transfer is to use icons throughout your materials. Icons can be used to indicate an action needed to the learner (for example, WWW Link, Group Activity, Important Tip, DVD disk). You can also use icons as guideposts to let your learners know where they are in a series of activities or steps. Icons also stand out from the content and draw attention to a shift in activity. Exhibit 5.4 show some sample icon sets.

Exhibit 5.4. Sample Icon Sets

Stay consistent: Are the colors within the color palette? Do the images use the same system? Are the page numbers in the same position? Are the fonts consistent according to headings? Consistent details make a big difference in the professionalism, usability, and impression the materials give.

Pay attention to detail: Go over the final materials with a fine-tooth comb. Have someone who has never seen your work go over the material as if he were part of the audience. Conduct separate reviews for content, format, and copyediting.

Use the right graphics: Choose graphics that can help explain your content visually. Use a "wheel" graphic when you are talking about a cycle. Use bar graphs when you are comparing numbers. Keep graphics simple and use your colors to emphasize your points. Do not use graphics just because you think you need one on every page. White space is not a bad thing. Not every page must be filled to the brim. Exhibit 5.5 is an example of how *not* to use graphics, as well as an example of a well-placed graphic.

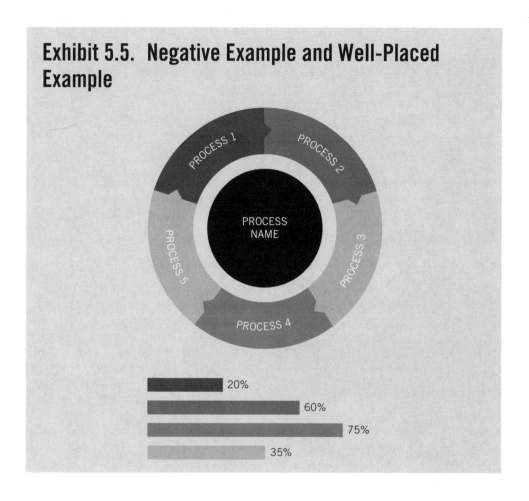

Exhibit 5.5. Negative Example and Well-Placed Example

Every one of these guidelines will help you create polished and effective training materials. Taking the time to make sure your materials support (rather than distract from) your content is critical to making sure they have a positive impact on your learner.

Next Steps

The next four chapters will help the course developer design specific training activities. Chapter 6 deals with writing activities that have a combination of learning objectives to acquire new information, build skills, and influence attitudes. Chapter 7 deals with writing activities to acquire knowledge; Chapter 8 deals with writing activities that develop skills; and Chapter 9 deals with writing activities that influence attitudes.

6

Develop Learning Activities to Acquire Knowledge and Skill and to Influence Attitudes

In this chapter, readers will find information about all kinds of activities, including:

- Application sharing

- Case studies

- Discussion and chat

- Games, exercises, simulations, and structured experiences

- In-basket exercises

- Interviews

- Jigsaw learning, teaching learning teams, and teaching projects

- Polling

- Task force projects

- Writing tasks

- Session starters and energizers

Tools

- 6.1. Application Sharing Debriefing Questions
- 6.2. Case Study Checklist
- 6.3. Case Study Critique Sheet
- 6.4. Customize a Case Study Worksheet
- 6.5. Debriefing Questions for Discussion Activities
- 6.6. Questions to Evaluate an Existing Game
- 6.7. Checklist for Designing Your Own Game
- 6.8. Processing Questions for Games and Simulations
- 6.9. Debriefing Questions for an In-Basket Activity
- 6.10. Jigsaw Learning/Team Teaching Debriefing Questions

Exhibits

- 6.1. The Dirty Dozen Game
- 6.2. Sample Interview: New Employee Orientation
- 6.3. Sample Team Teaching Project Instructions
- 6.4. Sample Action Plan
- 6.5. Sample Behavioral Skill Action Plan
- 6.6. Sample Action Plan Worksheet
- 6.7. Sample Supervisor's Help Action Plan
- 6.8. Sample Writing Assignment
- 6.9. Sample Visual Problem-Solving Activity
- 6.10. Sample Kinesthetic Problem-Solving Activity

The training methods in this chapter are very powerful and effective techniques because each method provides a combination of imparting knowledge, acquiring skills, and influencing the learners' attitudes. Use Tool 5.1 as your guide to develop learning materials for each method in this chapter.

Application Sharing

Think of application sharing as a cyber field trip. Learners are shown a digital application, software, or website for a specific purpose. Here is how to use Tool 5.1 as your guide to develop materials for this technique:

1. Identify the business need to develop specific training materials around this application. Begin to build a partnership with the manager of those who will attend the training session. Decide how to introduce the application with the help of the manager.

2. Identify the class where the application is shared. What is the primary focus of the class? What is the time limit of the class, if any?

3. Identify the target population. Who will be attending the program where the application is shared? How many at a time? Will different levels attend the class at the same time?

4. Write the learning objectives related to seeing this application: What do you want the learner to be able to do by the end of the session? Application sharing should inform, teach skills, and influence attitudes, opinions, or feelings. Your objectives are a combination of these three types of objectives.

5. Decide *how* you will evaluate whether learning objectives have been reached.

6. Identify the delivery medium (classroom training, online learning, blended mediums, etc.). Application sharing can be delivered in any of these settings.

7. Develop learner materials by adapting or modifying existing content or by creating the content, including visual aids. Most software applications have documentation that can be adapted for this purpose.

8. Identify instructions and questions for the five steps of adult learning to process the learning activity.

    - Set up each learning activity.

    - Complete the learning activity.

    - Learners share and interpret their reactions to the activities.

    - Learners identify concepts from their reactions.

    - Learners apply concepts to their situation.

    - Use Tool 6.1 to help write debriefing questions.

9. Use DIF analysis (Tool 4.6) to identify how much practice is required to learn this material.

10. Use the Methods Variety Scale (Tool 4.5) to pace the learner's activity level to avoid boredom.

11. Write a knowledge or skill test (activity) to identify to what extent the learning objectives have been met.

12. Develop a leader's guide.

Tool 6.1. Application Sharing Debriefing Questions

Learners to Share and Interpret Their Reactions to the Activity

- What happened when you tried out the application on your own?
- What surprised you?
- What part was easy? Difficult? What made it easy? Difficult?
- What did you notice/observe? How was that significant?
- How was that positive/negative?
- What struck you most about that?
- How do these pieces fit together?

Learners to Identify Concepts from Their Reactions

- How does this application relate to other parts of the process?
- What might we conclude from that?
- What did you learn/relearn?
- What processes/steps are similar to this one?
- What else is this step/process like?
- What does that suggest to you about _____ in general?
- What's important to remember about this application?
- What other functions impact the use of this application?

Learners to Apply Concepts to Their Situation

- How can you use this application most effectively?
- What is the value of this application to your job?
- What would be the consequence of doing/not doing this?
- What shortcuts can you use to help the application work for you?

The Case Study Method[1]

Trainers know that learners understand concepts and acquire skills faster when they participate in their own learning. Case studies are a great training method to increase participation, make learning more enjoyable, and enhance retention of knowledge and skills as well as influence learners' attitudes. So why aren't case studies used more often in training? One reason is that many trainers find it difficult to write a realistic case study that meets a clearly defined learning objective without identifying the "guilty" parties in their own organizations.

A case study is chosen by the trainer to present issues similar to the issues the learners are likely to encounter when trying to apply new knowledge and skills following a training program. A case study may be a paragraph, a page, or several pages. The amount of detail developed depends on the purpose of the case. A case study brings an element of realism to help the learner use and apply knowledge and skills. Case studies provide practice in diagnosing and solving problems and give ways to apply newly learned knowledge and practice skills.

Five Types of Case Studies

Typically, case studies are written for one of five purposes. These types of case studies are

1. *Identification:* This type of case study is appropriate to help learners identify both positive and negative characteristics of a situation. As part of the learning process, the learners are asked to find points similar to those that may be present in their own work lives. These provide a safer way to identify the characteristics or points from the case that they find in themselves.

2. *Problem Solving:* This type of case study helps the learners use systematic and creative problem-solving techniques. Problem-solving

---

[1]Adapted from *Instant Case Studies* © 2004 by Jean Barbazette, published by Pfeiffer, an Imprint of Wiley. Used with permission.

case studies can be used to have learners solve an entire problem using a specific problem-solving model or to have learners focus on any part of the problem-solving process, such as finding a solution or clearly identifying the problem.

3. *Practice:* This type of case study helps learners think about and use a new idea or try out a skill in a safe setting before using it in the real world. These case studies can also be used to help learners explore and clarify their attitudes about specific issues.

4. *Application:* This type of case study is often used at the end of a training program to summarize and review a set of complex ideas and skills to be presented during the program. Different elements of the case can address how the complex ideas that were learned are interrelated as well as show how to overcome obstacles to using new ideas and skills back on the job.

5. *Serial:* This type of case study uses an initial situation or set of characters and progressively adds new elements for the learners' consideration. Some of the elements from the above four types of cases may be used at different times during the workshop. This type of case study can save time because learners already understand the background of the case and can focus on the new element, idea, or skill being introduced. Another type of serial case study uses the same situation and asks the learners to apply different tools and skills.

Examples of the Five Types of Case Studies

The next few pages present examples of the five types of case studies described above. For each case study, the purpose is given, followed by instructions to the learners and questions to consider, explore, and discuss following independent reading of the case.

At the end of each case are questions for the facilitator to ask as he or she leads a discussion of that particular case. These questions are designed to complete the learning process by helping the learners identify the pertinent concepts and apply what is learned.

Identification Case Study Example: New Supervisor

The purpose of this diagnostic case study is for the learners to identify what a new supervisor is doing that is appropriate or inappropriate. After identifying these behaviors, a learner (a new supervisor) can determine what similar behaviors he or she is doing or not doing and how to be more successful.

Instructions: As you read the case below:

1. Underline the things you think Sue is doing correctly.

2. Bracket [ ] the things you think Sue is doing incorrectly.

3. Would you like Sue to work for you? Would you like to work for Sue?

Sue Weldon is a highly regarded charge nurse and a bit of a perfectionist. She was promoted into a supervisory position six months ago because she is one of the best surgical staff nurses at Medical Center.

Sue is a methodical planner and closely supervises the unit that helps patients recover from surgery. Sue says, "It's my job to get employees to provide the best patient care possible and do that in the most cost-effective manner possible. If anyone is doing something wrong, I tell him or her exactly what to do. I have learned to size up a problem quickly. I'm concerned about quality care for our patients. I have learned to get to the heart of the matter. My biggest problem is getting the rest of the staff to focus on care delivery. There's so much emphasis on cost containment. They must remember we're here to help patients recover from surgery and be well enough by the time they are discharged."

Upper management respects Sue for her good judgment. Sue tends to think through an issue and then make all of the decisions herself. Sue believes she is pretty good at selling her decisions to her staff. A major concern is losing authority over her staff, so she is loath to admit making a mistake. When an employee does an excellent job, Sue is quick to compliment him or her. She is often concerned about solving problems. When she finds the guilty party, her facts are listed in rapid-fire order, and her criticism can be sharp, often in front of others.

Employees complain that Sue seldom asks their opinions on anything. They feel neglected and ignored.

The unit rarely fails to meet its targets and always receives high marks on patient satisfaction surveys. To make sure productivity and satisfaction levels remain high, Sue frequently stays beyond the end of her shift to finish a job and complete planning tasks. Medical Center administration is pleased with Sue's unit, but the vice president of nursing is concerned that Sue is spending excessive overtime and that it could affect her health.

Facilitator Processing Questions

- What are the behaviors of an effective supervisor?
- What circumstances make it easy or difficult for a new supervisor to be effective with subordinates?
- How can a new supervisor overcome some of the barriers to supervising others?
- What characteristics are important for you to develop?
- How will you do that?

Problem-Solving Case Study Example: Rumors Abound!

The purpose of this case study is to solve a problem by identifying the problem, creating a plan, and then taking action. This case helps the learner sort out rumors from fact as part of the information-gathering step in problem solving.

Instructions: Create your plan of action to address the problem presented in the following case.

You have been hearing rumors that there are major complaints with the filing of correspondence in your department. Files everyone uses are missing, people waste hours of precious time trying to locate files, and the "sign-out" system is ignored by just about everyone. Because you work for the department manager, this issue has landed on your desk and your boss has told you to "fix it." When you begin to talk to others with access to the files, it is difficult to find anyone who has heard a complaint or is aware of the situation.

Facilitator Processing Questions

- What is the problem?

- What are the elements of the problem you want to uncover by your investigation?

- What actions will you take to resolve the problem of looking for missing files?

- Is your plan of action realistic?

- What problems might occur if you implemented this plan?

- What else could you do to solve this problem?

- Are those involved in the problem likely to accept your plan of action?

- What did you learn about planning to solve problems from this situation?

- What are you likely to do when faced with similar problems?

Practice Case Study Example: Giving Orders

The skill being practiced is supervising the work of others with the appropriate amount of direction. Orders can be given by offering information, making suggestions, making requests, or making commands. The case helps the learner read a problem all the way through to realize the possible consequences of some actions. The case also helps the learner recognize that effective direction is done with the *least* amount of control.

Instructions: Read the situation below and answer the five questions in preparation for discussion with others.

Your manager has asked you to arrange the conference room for an orientation to your company for a group of very important visitors. There will be about twenty people attending the meeting, and you want to make a good impression. Because several people's offices have been moved recently, the conference room has been used to store boxes. Making arrangements to clear the area is not part of your duties, but no one else is available at the moment.

You have asked two people to help you set up the room. One of them, Mary, is with you. She is your new support person. Jim, a custodian, has not shown up yet. The meeting will take place in two hours. In addition to some heavy cartons, the room is overcrowded with chairs and is dusty. You envision seating the visitors around the conference table. A slide presentation will be shown on the front wall; no screen is available.

1. You have an idea of how you want to arrange the room. Write down exactly what you would say to Mary in one sentence.

2. You decide to first clear the area for the projector. You want Mary to help you move some heavy cartons. What do you say to Mary?

3. After you have been dusting chairs off for 20 minutes, Jim shows up. Working has been difficult because the room is overcrowded with cartons. What do you say to Jim?

4. Jim is trying to lift a heavy carton by himself, instead of asking for help or using a hand truck (which is downstairs). You are concerned Jim will hurt his back. What do you say?

5. Finally, the room looks as it should. You sit down in one of the chairs to rest a bit and notice that the wall directly opposite the projector has an electrical box in the center of it. It will be impossible to show the presentation on that wall. The table will have to be moved down and the projector moved to the other end of the room. What do you say to Jim and Mary?

Facilitator Processing Questions

- What made it easy or difficult to find the right words to give orders to a new support person?

- How is giving instructions different when the person receiving your instructions doesn't report to you?

- What did you learn about giving instructions from this case study?

Application Case Study Example: Prioritize Training Projects

Prior to reading this case study, the learners have studied skills for managing a training function in a two-day workshop. The case helps the training manager apply a variety of skills, including identifying training needs, prioritizing projects, allocating resources, budgeting for training, and building alliances in the operation.

Instructions: Review the set of circumstances and conditions described in the case below and then answer these questions:

- What are your *objectives* for training?

- What is your recommendation to the vice president of operations (your boss)?

Include recommendations for:

- The type of training

- Target population

- Delivery system (centralized versus road trip for general office trainer, self-paced video, outside seminars, train store managers as trainers, etc.)

- The number of people you need to add to your staff of three (a course designer, an instructor, a support person)

You are the training manager of "Catch Us Now," a small fast-food chain that specializes in seafood. You have twenty-five outlets in Southern California, Nevada, and Arizona. The general office is in Southern California. The company has committed to opening one new store per month for twenty-four months—the size will double in two years.

Cashier/counter server turnover is 60 percent. Currently, store managers barely have the time to interview cashiers, let alone train them. They are begging for help in recruitment and training of cashiers/servers. Of the 40 percent who remain, some feel promotions go to those with connections in high places. They feel they are the "workhorses" who hold the company together.

New store managers are promoted from within. The average age of store managers is twenty-seven. The regional manager does training for new store managers on an as-needed basis. Two years ago, a manual was developed on how to run and manage a store. It needs to be updated.

Each store has about twenty cashier/counter servers and cooks. Brief job descriptions exist for each position, but procedure manuals are very brief. No effective orientation program exists.

About eight months ago the store managers completed a mandatory interviewing seminar. The chain is still experiencing several problems from "bad" hires. Grievances are still at too high a rate. Little improvement has come about in this area.

You are suspicious that the interviewing class may not have been as effective as you would have liked. The managers were enthusiastic, but the interviewing class was mostly lecture. It began with scare tactics about previous lawsuits and losses the company has suffered because of bad hires. The managers received handout materials that gave "chapter and verse" about legal questions to ask; but this material was gone over quickly and mostly included for "reference."

Answer the questions in the instructions at the beginning of the case study.

Facilitator Processing Questions

- What information led you to decide how to prioritize these training issues?

- How do the proposed recommendations support the objectives you developed for this situation?

- What additional information needs to be developed to allow you to finish the plan?

- What did you learn about prioritizing training issues from this case?

- How will you use these skills in the future?

Serial Case Study Example: Manager's Role

The purpose of this type of case study is to develop a series of skills by adding information to an ongoing situation. In the first part of the case study, the training manager plans to build a partnership with the managers of the learners who will attend training. The training manager identifies what needs to be done before, during, and after the training. After additional skills are learned, the case situation is revisited two more times to apply skills being taught in the training manager workshop. Progressive case studies have the advantage of building on previous information, and added information helps bring sophistication and nuances to learning.

Part 1

Instructions: Read the information about the business need, training plan, and target population and then identify appropriate tasks and roles for the store manager before, during, and after Product Knowledge Training.

Situation: Fine jewelry retail chain requests training for retail associates. *The business need* for a fine jewelry store chain is to increase retail sales, particularly on higher-priced products.

The training plan calls for interactive *product knowledge* training for retail associates. The training was designed at the corporate office in half-day modules to be conducted at the Regional Training Centers by corporate trainers assigned to each region. Role-play practice to sell higher-priced products is included in each module. A prerequisite for the product knowledge training is completion of selling skills training, conducted monthly at the Regional Training Centers. Not all retail associates have attended selling skills training. Some managers say their stores are short-staffed and don't have the coverage to release new associates to attend training outside the store.

The target population is two groups of retail associates: (1) sophisticated and experienced at selling fine jewelry (average age thirty-eight) or (2) young and inexperienced (average age twenty-four). This younger group finds selling expensive jewelry difficult because they cannot afford such products for themselves.

If the chain is to meet the business need, identify the appropriate roles and tasks for the store managers before, during and after product knowledge training.

Facilitator Processing Questions

- What roles and tasks did you identify for the store managers before, during, and after product knowledge training?

- What helped or hindered you in identifying these roles?

- What additional information do you need to better identify these roles?

- In general, what does a store manager need to do to support a training effort to achieve the desired results from training?

- In your organization, what can be done to encourage managers to support a training effort to produce the desired results?

Part 2

Instructions: Based on Part 1 of the case study, identify the changes in knowledge, attitude, and individual behavior that need to take place *with store managers* in order for their associates' learning to transfer to the workplace.

Knowledge Changes

Attitude Changes

Behavior Changes

Next, answer the following about the store managers:

1. Identify their probable level of commitment to the changes:

    ____ Commitment (eager dedication, initiative, and willing participation)

    ____ Genuine compliance (willingness and agreement with goals at the direction of others)

    ____ Formal compliance (will complete as part of one's job)

    ____ Grudging compliance (will complete only to keep a job)

    ____ Non-compliance (not willing)

2. What amount of resistance is likely to occur that could be a barrier to transfer?

3. Which strategies will be critical to overcome that resistance?

4. What other strategies do you suggest that have not been discussed previously?

Facilitator Processing Questions

- Given the changes in knowledge, attitude, and behavior that have just been discussed, what might it take to increase the managers' commitment and reduce resistance to change?

- How realistic are the strategies to overcome resistance by store managers?

- What are the characteristics of helpful strategies to overcome resistance to change by managers?

- What can be done to overcome resistance to change by managers in your organization?

Part 3

Instructions: Using the information from Parts 1 and 2 of the case study, identify the changes in knowledge, attitude, and individual behavior that need to take place *for the retail associates* in order for their learning to transfer to the workplace.

Knowledge Changes

Attitude Changes

Behavior Changes

Answer the following about the learners (store associates):

1. Identify their probable level of commitment to these changes:

    ___ Commitment

    ___ Genuine compliance

    ___ Formal compliance

    ___ Grudging compliance

    ___ Non-compliance

2. What kind of resistance is likely to occur that could be a barrier to transfer?

3. Which manager strategies will be critical to overcome that resistance?

5. What other strategies do you suggest that have not been discussed previously?

Facilitator Processing Questions

*   Given the changes that the retail associates need to make and their level of commitment, how realistic are the strategies to overcome resistance to these changes?

*   What differences are there between strategies to overcome resistance of managers and their subordinates?

*   What have you learned about overcoming resistance and effective strategies through the three progressive case studies?

*   How can these strategies be applied in your organization?

Where Case Studies Fit in Workshop Design

Prior to writing or customizing an existing case study for inclusion in a specific training program, basic elements of training program design must be followed. A business need should be established for conducting the training. The course designer must complete a target population assessment to gather information about the needs of the group and their prior knowledge, skill level, and experience with the subject of the training program. Also, the course designer must perform a job/task analysis to determine the best way to complete the work. Once learning objectives are written and a course content outline developed, the course designer can select a variety of interactive methods to meet the learning objectives. A means of measuring the outcomes of the training program must also be developed as part of the process.

When the course developer decides using a case study is the most appropriate method of reaching the learning objective, follow the eight-step method below to write an original case study or customize a case for inclusion in a training program.

How to Develop a Case Study

There are eight steps in case study development.

1. Write a learning objective.

2. Select a type of case study based on the objective.

3. Select the setting and characters required to reach the objective.

4. Add dialogue if appropriate.

5. Write instructions and discussion questions.

6. Test the case study and obtain feedback.

7. Revise the case study based on feedback.

8. Develop variations.

Following is a description of the eight steps in case study development. Three templates (Tools 6.2, 6.3, and 6.4) to make case study development easier follow the description.

1. Write a Learning Objective

Here is a sample learning objective for the Identification case study example above. After discussing the case study in a small group [objective condition], the supervisors [objective written from learner's point of view] will be able to identify behaviors and characteristics of an effective supervisor [describes specific behavior] and list three appropriate steps to increase personal effectiveness as a supervisor [identifies the level of achievement, quality and quantity].

When you use adjectives like "appropriate" to describe the level of achievement, have a model in mind. Define words like appropriate; and help the learners discover the model as part of their discussion. In this case study, an appropriate strategy to increase personal effectiveness would include a strategy to overcome one or more pitfalls of new supervisors.

2. Select a Type of Case Study Based on the Objective

After writing a specific learning objective for the case study, decide which of the five types of case studies will best help the learners to discover the concept or learning point. Below are several questions that will help you select the right type of case study:

Identification

- What characteristics or points will be identified?

- Will both positive and negative characteristics be identified as part of the learning process?

- As part of the learning process, will the learner be asked to identify the characteristics or points from the case that they find in themselves?

Problem Solving

- What is the problem the learner is to solve?

- What problem-solving model will be used to solve the problem?

- What problem-solving skills do the target population already have that they can apply to this issue?

- Will elements of systematic and creative problem-solving techniques be used in the case?

- What steps in the problem-solving process do the learners complete? For example, will the problem be identified for the learner so the learner focuses on finding a solution, or is part of the case study to clearly identify the problem?

Practice

- What skills will the learners practice?

- What new ideas are the learners to discuss?

- Which attitudes is the case intended to influence?

- What is the sequence of multiple skills?

- Will the learners be able to identify assumptions made by the characters in the case?

- Will the learners be asked to identify prerequisites as a part of the practice?

Application

- What are the elements to summarize and apply a set of complex ideas and/or skills that appear in this case?

- How are the elements of the case related to each other?

- Is the sequence of elements an issue in this case?

- Will learners prioritize the elements of the case to demonstrate what has been learned?

- What is the setting in which the learners will apply a set of complex ideas or skills?

Serial

- Which elements from the above four types of cases can be combined to develop a progression of skills?

- What is the progression of elements that will be developed?

- Will the case study developer need to use a task analysis and skill hierarchy to help sequence the progression of ideas, concepts, and skills?

3. Select the Setting and Characters Required to Reach the Objective

After writing an objective and selecting the appropriate type of case study, select the setting and characters that are likely to help learners to reach the learning objective. Consider a setting that closely parallels the learners' situation. Factors include:

- Where learners work: industry, government or non-profit organization

- Reporting relationships: type of work groups or team environment

- Collective bargaining organization or not

- Size and scope of the setting

- Physical setting

Industry-specific settings help the learners easily identify with the situation. For example, employees in a manufacturing setting prefer to read case studies set in a manufacturing plant that resembles their workplace. Successful settings also resemble reporting relationships. For example, employees who work in a team environment usually have a "team leader" rather than a supervisor found in a work group with a more rigid hierarchy. Those who work in a "union shop" prefer case studies that mirror their environment. The size and scope of the setting refers to whether a case is set in an organization, a division, a department, a work group, or between two individuals. If the physical setting makes a difference, it would describe the location of the interaction that is the focus of the case study. For example, a bank employee could meet the customer on a teller line, at the drive-up teller window, or on the telephone. The interaction between two individuals might take place in an office, on the shop floor, at the customer's place of business, or in the break room. When choosing the setting, it needs to parallel the learners' situation so the learners can focus on the learning point and not be distracted with an unfamiliar setting.

When selecting characters for a case study, consider whether these elements make sense in reaching the learning objective of a particular case:

- Job titles of characters

- Age, gender, and cultural background of characters

- Whether to give names to characters

- Knowledge, skills, and attitudes of characters

Effective job titles parallel the learners' experience. If sales clerks are called "associates" in the learners' workplace, call them "associates" in the case study. If most of the target population reading a case study are Hispanic females in their fifties, then make the characters familiar to the audience by creating a character with those attributes. Learners ought to be able to identify with the characters in the case as typical of their situation.

Create characters who are believable without specific individuals being recognizable. Names ought to reflect those typical in the organization. If a character does not have a name, refer to the character by job title. Be careful not to use stereotypes or show ethnic bias in selecting and naming characters.

4. Add Dialogue If Appropriate

Writing dialogue that sounds natural is difficult. If your dialogue is believable and typical of the character and contributes to the purpose of the case, then use it. If you think the dialogue does not sound natural or authentic or might distract learners, leave it out. Effective case studies usually come from developing the setting and the characters, rather than the words the characters say.

5. Write Instructions and Discussion Questions

Write instructions for the reader to prepare for a discussion. Written instructions at the beginning of the case study tell the learners what to look for or what to prioritize or in some way judge the information that follows. For example, the identification case study above asked the reader to "Underline the things you think Sue is doing correctly. Bracket the things you think Sue is doing incorrectly. Decide whether you would like Sue to work for you. Would you like to work for Sue?" Repeat the same questions at the end of the case study if you expect the learners to answer them in writing prior to a discussion.

After the learners discuss the case study questions, ask additional questions to develop and apply the concepts. Write questions for the facilitator to ask. These questions are called "Facilitator Processing Questions" throughout this book. The five sample case studies in this chapter 1 have some processing questions. Also see Tools 6.5, 6.8, 6.9, and 6.10 for questions.

6. Test the Case Study and Obtain Feedback

Write a test scenario for the case study. Is it realistic without being too close to home? Will the learners achieve the learning objective or understand the purpose of the case through the setting and characters? Are questions appropriately worded to encourage discussion of relevant issues? Is the dialogue between characters helpful rather than distracting? Have both peers (others who know something about case study construction) and target population given feedback on the case. A template of a critique sheet to assess the effectiveness of a case study is presented in Tool 6.3.

7. Revise the Case Study Based on Feedback

Based on feedback from peers and the target population, identify changes that are appropriate for the case study. You do not need to implement every suggestion. Sometimes suggested revisions are a matter of style, rather than substance. Identify those revisions that make sense and will actually improve the case study.

8. Develop Variations

Finally, consider creating different versions of the same case study so you can use it in another course with a few changes. For example, several departments may be attending the same workshop and, by changing the setting to another department, you can use the case study effectively for a different target population. See Tool 6.4 for customizing a case study.

Overcoming Problems When Developing Case Studies

When developing or customizing a case study, pay attention to these types of problems:

- Too much detail
- Too many points cause confusion
- Too close to reality (people and/or situation)

Learners frequently need fewer details than in the real situation to meet the learning objective. If the objective of the case study can be accomplished in one paragraph instead of three and still make the same point, use one paragraph. Too many details about a situation can cause confusion and divert attention from the points that need to be discussed.

The purpose of the first three types of case studies (diagnostic, problem solving, and practice) is to help learners discuss one aspect of an issue. Narrow the setting and the characters to focus on the specific point the learners are to discover. When case studies focus on several points, learners can become confused and may spend discussion time sorting out several pieces of information that will not help them reach the learning objective. It is often easier to write two or three serial case studies than combine all the points into one complex case study.

Keep in mind that a case study needs to be natural, familiar, and authentic while *not* duplicating the real situation. To create characters who are believable without being able to recognize the identity of specific individuals, combine several attributes into the same character or change the age, gender, or physical attributes of the character. The combination of attributes makes the character easier to discuss, and the learners will recognize the purpose of the case more easily. When learners recognize characters or a specific situation, the learning point is often forgotten and case study discussions can become gossip sessions.

Three templates are provided to help the case study developer use the suggestions in this chapter:

- Tool 6.2. Case Study Checklist (eight steps to write a case study).

- Tool 6.3. Case Study Critique (a point system to identify weak areas needing to be redesigned)

- Tool 6.4. Customize a Case Study Worksheet (to redesign an existing case study)

Tool 6.2. Case Study Checklist

Use this eight-step process to write a case study:

1. Write a learning objective. "Given a case study, the _____ [insert learner's job title] will be able to _____ [insert specific behavior], and _____ [insert the level of achievement: quality, quantity or speed].

2. Select one of the five types of case studies based on the objective:

   • Identification

   • Problem solving

   • Practice

   • Application

   • Serial

3. Select the setting and characters needed to reach the objective.

Setting

   • Where learners work: industry, government, or non-profit organization

   • Reporting relationships: type of work groups or team environment

   • Collective bargaining organization or not

   • Size and scope of the setting

   • Physical setting

Characters

   • Job titles of characters

   • Age, gender, and cultural differences of characters

   • Whether to give names to characters

   • Knowledge, skills, and attitudes of characters

Tool 6.2. Case Study Checklist *(continued)*

4. Add dialogue if appropriate.

5. Write instructions and discussion questions, including:

   - Clear instructions to set up the case study

   - Specific questions to answer as the case is discussed

   - Appropriate facilitator questions to process learning points

6. Test the case study and obtain feedback.

7. Revise the case study based on feedback.

8. Develop variations.

Tool 6.3. Case Study Critique Sheet

Instructions: Read the case study and rate the completeness of each element based on the following scale:

0 = element is absent
1 = minimal element or confused information
2 = sufficient information
3 = appropriate information

_____ Learning objective has all four elements (written from learner's point of view, specific behavior, condition, and level of achievement).

_____ Appropriate type of case study selected. If not appropriate, suggest a different type of case study: _____ (identification, problem solving, practice, application, serial)

_____ Setting specific enough to reach the objective (industry, reporting relationships, union/non-union, size/scope, physical setting)

_____ Characters specific enough to reach the objective (job titles, age, gender, cultural differences, names of characters, knowledge, skills, attitudes represented)

_____ Dialogue appropriate

_____ Instructions clear

_____ Questions for learners are appropriate

_____ Facilitator questions are appropriate and develop learning points

_____ **Total Points** (total scores under 14 need revision to achieve the objective)

Tool 6.3. Case Study Critique Sheet *(continued)*

Suggested revisions to this case:

Tool 6.4. Customize a Case Study Worksheet

Case studies can be more effective when used with a new target audience by customizing the setting, characters, dialogue, instructions, and questions. Use this form when considering points to customize for an existing case study. Answer these questions about the new target audience:

_____ Is the *learning objective* the same as in the existing case? If not, is this the appropriate case study for the learning point that participants will discover?

_____ Is the *type of case study* appropriate for the new target audience? Is a different type of case more appropriate?

_____ What parts of the setting have to be customized? Is the setting too close to reality?

- Where learners work

- Reporting relationships

- Collective bargaining setting or not

- Size and scope of the case

- Physical setting

_____ What elements of the case characters should be customized? Are they too close to reality?

- Job titles of characters

- Age, gender, cultural differences

- Characters' names

- Knowledge, skills, and attitudes of characters

_____ What parts of the dialogue should be customized?

_____ What parts of the instructions have to be customized?

_____ What discussion questions have to be customized or added?

_____ What facilitator questions have to be customized or added?

Debriefing Questions for the Five Types of Case Studies

When writing a case study, choose appropriate questions for the learners to answer that will lead to the point the learners are to discover through the case study. Consider selecting these types of discussion questions for each type of case study and make the questions part of the instructions:

Identification

- What is the person in the case doing correctly/incorrectly?

- What problems result from how the person in the case handles each issue?

- What other approaches do you recommend to be more effective?

Problem Solving

- What is the main problem?

- What are the symptoms of the problem versus causes of the problem?

- Are there issues that may not be problems and do not require your attention?

- What are the possible solutions in this case?

- What are the advantages/disadvantages of each solution?

- What is your plan of action?

- What do you recommend?

Practice

- What is the skill you are using?

- How easy/difficult is it to use this skill?

- What makes it easy or difficult to use this skill?

- What helps or hinders you using these ideas or skills?

- What are the problems you encounter when trying out this skill?

- How can you overcome the difficulties in using this skill?

- What are the building blocks to using this skill?

- If you are willing to re-evaluate your attitude toward this skill, what is another perspective you have gained in using it?

Application

- What are the key points in making this issue successful?

- How are the key points interrelated?

- What are the critical elements of success?

- What are the barriers to being successful?

- How can you overcome these barriers?

- How can you prioritize the lesson learned from this case for your situation?

- What are the consequences of not paying attention to primary issues in this case?

- What skills help you overcome the barriers in this case?

- How will you realistically apply this skill in your setting?

Serial

- How do successive knowledge, skills, and attitudes build upon each other?

- What insights have you gained from successive knowledge or skills in this case?

- Given hindsight, what could you have done sooner to be more successful in solving the issues of this case?

Facilitator Processing Questions

After learners have discussed the questions about the learning points in the case study, the facilitator must ask additional questions to meet the learning objective. Learners have to reflect on the case study and share their reactions with each other as a transition step to move from the case situation to recognizing what they have learned. Once general concepts have been learned, participants can then apply what is learned to their own situations. Facilitator processing questions are not shown to the learner as part of the case study; rather they are given to the facilitator as part of a lesson plan with suggested answers.

Here are several questions to facilitate discussing learning points:

For Learners to Share and Interpret Their Reactions to the Activity

- What happened when you tried out that function/step as part of the case?

- What surprised you?

- What part was easy? Difficult? What made it easy? Difficult?

- What did you notice/observe? How was that significant?

- How was that positive/negative?

- What struck you most about that?

- How do these pieces fit together?

For Learners to Identify Concepts from Their Reactions

- How does this relate to other parts of the process?

- What might we conclude from that?

- What did you learn/relearn?

- What processes/steps are similar to this one?

- What else is this step/process like?

- What does that suggest to you about _____ in general?

- What's important to remember about this step/function?

- What other options/ways do you have for completing this step/function?

- How can you integrate this step into the larger process?

- What other functions are impacted by this step?

For Learners to Apply Concepts to Their Situation

- How can you use this?

- What is the value of this step/function?

- What would be the consequence of doing/not doing this?

- What changes can you make to help it work for you?

- How does that fit with your experience?

Discussion or Chat

Discussion or chat (used in online learning) is an opportunity for learners to discuss issues, share ideas and opinions in a group, or post comments in a threaded discussion. How to develop inquiry-oriented discussions is covered in Chapter 9, along with other techniques that influence the learners' attitudes. Three types of questions help the instructor facilitate a discussion: open, closed, and follow-up.

Use closed questions to clarify a point and to direct or control a discussion. Closed questions can be answered adequately in a *few* words. Closed questions help participants make identifications or selections as well as answer simple "yes" or "no" questions. For example:

- What kind of machine is this?

- Who is responsible for distributing this form?

- Do you think closed or open questions are better at promoting discussion?

- Who is right, the supervisor or the trainee?

- Does preparing the lesson plan come before setting learning objectives?

- Is the first step in problem solving to find the facts?

Many closed questions begin with are, can, was, did, do, which, or when.

Open questions require *more than a few words* to answer adequately. Use open questions to explore a rationale, gain greater insight into a participant's contribution, help apply a learning point, or elicit more information to solve a problem. Open questions are subjective when focusing on opinions and can be objective when focusing on factual information. For example,

- What do you think about that?

- Why should Alex lead the group?

- Why do you think the teller found the error?

- What evidence did the police have?

- How have you been handling the process until now?

- What factors are necessary in a good training situation?

- What should the supervisor do now?

- How would you implement the five steps we just discussed?

Open questions begin with what, why, or how.

Be aware that open questions require preparation by the participants prior to answering them. Participants can become defensive when asked open questions that start with *why.* Open questions that begin with what or how are often easier for them to answer.

If you want to reach the learning objective and help the instructor encourage more participation, write follow-up questions to initial open questions. Use follow-up questions to clarify or help the learners understand the original question, to expand, probe, or dig more deeply into the same idea, or obtain additional ideas. For example:

- What are other examples of that?

- What else has happened when you completed that step?

- Why do you think that happened?

- Has anyone else had that same or a similar experience?

- Tell me more about that.

Use Tool 6.5 as a template to help develop debriefing questions for discussion activities.

Tool 6.5. Debriefing Questions for Discussion Activities

Learners to Share and Interpret Their Reactions to the Activity

- What happened when you tried to express your ideas and opinions?

- What surprised you about the points raised by others?

- How was that positive/negative?

- What struck you most about the major discussion points?

- How do these pieces fit together?

Learners to Identify Concepts from Their Reactions

- How does this discussion relate to other parts of the work you do?

- What might we conclude from that?

- What did you learn/relearn?

- What's important to remember about this discussion?

- What new information did you learn?

- Have you changed from your original position?

Learners to Apply Concepts to Their Situation

- How can you use this points made in this discussion most effectively?

- What is the value of this discussion to your job?

- What would be the consequence of using/not using these ideas?

Games and Simulations[2]

Many different types of games and simulations can be used during a training session to promote skill development. Games and simulations are sometimes called activities, exercises, or structured experiences. Games differ from learning tournaments described in Chapter 6 because games usually teach more than information and require skill demonstrations. Consider using game formats from familiar quiz shows or board games. Most participants are familiar with the rules and with how these games are played. You can easily insert workshop content into this format. Some games are available on software. See the Bibliography for references.

Once you have decided to use a game as a learning method, decide whether you will use an existing game and modify it or create a new game. When selecting a game, follow the suggestions in Tool 6.6.

If you decide to create a new game, see the suggestions in Tool 6.7.

---

[2]Adapted from *The Art of Great Training Delivery* © 2007 by Jean Barbazette, published by Pfeiffer, an Imprint of Wiley. Used with permission.

Tool 6.6. Questions to Evaluate an Existing Game

- What is your learning objective?
- What is the sequence for the game with other materials?
- What is the game's objective?
- Does the game achieve the learning point you want to make?
- Are the instructions clear?
- Are the rules the same as the way this game is usually played?
- What is the setting or setup for the game?
- What materials are required?
- What is the degree of risk for participants?
- Is the payoff worth the time spent on the game?
- Does the game suggest variations to include your group?
- Will your learners be motivated to participate?
- What are the prerequisites?
- Is the complexity of the game process appropriate?
- Are your skills adequate to process the results of the game?
- Does the game require a referee, observer, or feedback?
- What are the costs?

Tool 6.7. Checklist for Designing Your Own Game

1. Write behavioral objectives.

2. Decide whether a game is the best method to meet the learning objectives.

3. Determine what kind of format for the game is best (puzzle, exercise, board game, etc.).

4. Review existing resources.

5. Follow selection/evaluation suggestions in Exhibit 6.5.

6. Write the learning point you want to make.

7. Identify the learners' motives to participate in the game.

8. Identify those who might resist involvement in the activity. What is the source of the resistance and how will you overcome it?

9. Identify how much risk is involved for the learners.

10. Create the instructions needed to introduce the game.

11. Identify characters, situation, or setting for the game.

12. Decide what participants *do* to meet the objective (look at a picture, answer questions, discuss learning points, come to consensus, interview each other, write thoughts for reflection, etc.).

13. Write instructions to read in class or for the learners to read themselves.

14. Estimate the time to "play" the game sufficiently to develop learning points.

15. Determine whether there a balance between learning and fun and between skill and luck.

16. Make the rules clear and easy to follow. Define what a player can or cannot do, how a score is kept, and what constitutes winning the game.

17. Use tokens or game pieces that are familiar and easily available.

18. Write questions to process the game using the five steps of adult learning.

19. Estimate the time to process the game.

20. Obtain feedback on design of the game from peers.

21. Test run or pilot the game with a target audience.

22. Evaluate to what extent the game objectives were met.

23. Identify learning points made that you did not anticipate.

24. Identify changes and/or variations for next time.

Here are some game formats and suggestions for the best uses of each:

Quiz shows are active, participative games played by either individuals or teams modeled after familiar television game shows. The objective or purpose of quiz shows is to recall facts and information that learners will need to memorize when use of a job aid is not realistic. Other objectives of quiz show games are to reinforce and review key points in a summary or update existing information as a session starter. Games can be used to help learners practice new skills by applying information correctly.

Examples, uses, and variations of quiz shows include recall or multiple-choice games like "Jeopardy," "Who Wants to Be a Millionaire," or "Hollywood Squares." These games can be played by individuals or teams. This format takes a lot of work to develop appropriate questions and answers. Common uses for these recall games include new employee orientation, policies and procedure training, and management training.

Board games like Bingo can ask employees to earn a space on a card by correctly answering questions or perform a skill. Board games are used to recall knowledge or demonstrate skills. For example, a card is drawn that directs a player to "do" a task such as format a disk in computer training or locate a fire extinguisher in an orientation session. Other objectives include applying new knowledge, learning new materials, or reinforcing learning principles during a summary of key points. Examples of board games include Bingo, Trivial Pursuit, Monopoly, and Tic-Tac-Toe.

Decision-making games and simulations imitate a real concept in a low-risk environment. They can be valuable training tools. Decision-making games are particularly good at helping learners identify their style and skill in making business decisions. Decision-making games can focus on individual decisions or group decisions, quick decisions, or considered and studied decisions. Often learners follow their first instincts during such games. Debriefing discussions help the learners identify the difference in results between following a first instinct or learning new decision-making skills.

Objectives and learning points taught by decision-making games include identifying the value and validity of individual decisions versus group decisions; identifying the difference between quick versus considered decisions; predicting how one acts during a crisis; and looking for competencies within a group. Decision-making games can be used in team building, supervisory training, and interpersonal skills classes. Examples of decision-making games include wilderness survival such as Marooned[3] or Outback,[4] and Clue. The Dirty Dozen, shown in Exhibit 6.1, is a decision-making game. It requires recalling information and applying it successfully.

Tool 6.8 is a list of questions to process games and simulations through adult learning steps 3, 4, and 5.

Exhibit 6.1. The Dirty Dozen Game
Dirty Dozen Game Handout

When the instructions are given to begin, underline the correctly spelled word in each pair.

Round 1	Round 2
1. similar/similiar	1. cemetery/cemetary
2. admissible/admissable	2. hypocrisy/hypocracy
3. miniture/miniature	3. sieze/seize
4. rebuttle/rebuttal	4. nickle/nickel
5. cooly/coolly	5. liquefy/liquify
6. massacre/massacer	6. alright/all right
7. suffrage/sufferage	7. asinine/assinine
8. ukulele/ukelele	8. apparrel/apparel
9. heroes/heros	9. pavilion/pavillion
10. quizzes/quizes	10. occasionally/occasionaly
11. restaurant/restraunt	11. parallel/paralell
12. hitchhiker/hitchiker	12. alotted/allotted

---

[3]HRDQ, King of Prussia, PA www.hrdq.com

[4]HRDQ, King of Prussia, PA. www.hrdq.com.

Dirty Dozen Game Instructions

Purpose: The following game teaches essential components of *group deci-sion making.*

1. *Instructor sets up the learning activity.* Have the participants form groups of *at least* three. Round I needs to have a sense of rush and urgency. Pull them together quickly and keep participants standing up.

2. *Round 1.* Participant groups have 20 seconds to decide which word in the pair of words is correctly spelled. After 20 seconds, call time and give the correct answers. Ask each group to report its score.

3. *Round 2.* Allow 2 minutes for the groups to select the correct answers. Most groups will not need this long, but ask them to take the full amount of time. After 2 minutes, call time and give the correct answers and record scores.

4. *Learners share and interpret their reactions to the activity.* Ask each group to list three things they did differently in their group between Rounds 1 and 2. Share group reports. Compare scores in the two rounds by asking which round obtained better results? How do group members feel about how the decisions were made each time?

5. *Learners identify concepts from their reactions.* Ask participants to move away from the word lists and discuss and list critical ele-ments in group decision making learned from their group processes. You may want to involve the group in a discussion of successful ver-sus effective decision making. *Successful* decision making means the group had the right answer. *Effective* decision making means everyone in the group felt good about the process. Discuss which focus is better for the objectives of the group—quick, correct deci-sions or long-term relations in a work group.

6. *Learners apply concepts to their situations.* Have participants write how they can use the new information and the concepts learned. Discuss, in the large group, application ideas and action items to relate the learning to the work environment.

Tool 6.8. Processing Questions for Games and Simulations

Learners Share and Interpret Reactions to Games and Simulations

- What helped you to be successful?
- What held back your progress?
- What surprised you about this game?
- Which results are significant?
- Was there a turning point in the game?

Learners Identify the Concept from a Game or Simulation

- What is the point that this game teaches?
- How can you integrate this new information into how you view your team?
- What did you learn about yourself that is significant?
- What is important for you to remember about how the game was played?
- What areas of your work will be most impacted by the results of this game?

Learners Apply What Is Learned from the Game or Simulation

- How will you use this information to build rapport with your team?
- What is the consequence of ignoring this information?
- To what extent does this game reflect your work life reality?
- How will you use the results of this game?
- Based on what you learned about yourself and your team from this game, what changes will you make?
- What barriers will you address that were identified by the game?

In-Basket Exercises

During an in-basket exercise, learners review typical paperwork to sort, delay, discard, or act on immediately. If a desk reference manual exists for the tasks you are teaching, be sure it is up-to-date. Be sure all the functions are represented that the employees are likely to experience in a normal work day. Write a learning objective for the exercise. Using DIF Analysis (Tool 4.6), identify how frequently each piece of paperwork is likely to appear. Consult Tool 5.1 for the remaining steps to design this exercise. Use Tool 6.9 to debrief the exercise.

Tool 6.9. Debriefing Questions for an In-Basket Activity

Learners to Share and Interpret Their Reactions to the Activity

- What happened when you first tried to sort out the different types of paperwork on your own?
- What surprised you?
- What part was easy? Difficult? What made it easy? Difficult?
- What did you notice/observe? How was that significant?
- How was that positive/negative?
- What struck you most about that?
- How do these pieces of paperwork fit together?

Learners to Identify Concepts from Their Reactions

- How does this paperwork relate to other parts of this job?
- What might we conclude from that?
- What did you learn/relearn?
- What processes/steps are similar to this one?
- What else is this step/process like?
- What does that suggest to you about paperwork processing in general?
- What's important to remember about this in-basket exercise?

Learners to Apply Concepts to Their Situation

- How can you use what you learned from this activity most effectively?
- What is the value of this in-basket exercise to your job?
- What would be the consequence of doing/not doing these paperwork tasks?
- What shortcuts can you use to help the paperwork processing tasks work for you?

Interviews

Interview activities help learners demonstrate skill in asking questions, evaluate and respond to another's answers, and gain feedback on their own development. To develop a successful interview activity, first identify the learning objective. Think about the setting for the interview. Will the interview be one-on-one or a group interview by a panel of experts? Will the interview be in person, on the telephone, through email, or threaded discussion? Next, estimate the length of time needed for the interview. Remember, an inexperienced learner might need more time to plan questions and receive developmental feedback. Next, write sample questions that reflect the dimensions you want the learner to "discover." Identify criteria for who ought to be answering the interview questions. Tell the respondent answering the questions the type of information he or she should offer and whether to freely offer information or make the person asking the questions probe for deeper answers. Next, write instructions for how a learner is to set up and conduct the interview. Give enough background information so the learner knows which skills are to be demonstrated during the conversation. Finally, test the interview questions by asking a peer to identify what type of answers are likely to be given to the questions and make revisions as needed.

Exhibit 6.2 if an example of an interview for a new employee to conduct during the process of orientation. This interview shows typical questions asked in an interview by a new employee of a co-worker, an internal customer, or a supervisor. This format has been most successful in orienting a staff or professional person who will have many contacts throughout the organization.

Exhibit 6.2. Sample Interview: New Employee Orientation

Interview objective: As you interview a co-worker, internal customer, or supervisor, develop information that will be useful to you as you form a working relationship with this person. Typically, this type of interview takes between 15 and 30 minutes.

Ask these questions and probe for deeper answers as needed:

- What is the main purpose of your job?
- Describe the occasions when we might be working together.
- When we work together, what do you expect from me?
- When we work together, what can I expect from you?
- What are past problems that have occurred when working with someone from my department; and how can similar problems be avoided in the future?

Following the interview, debrief the activity by using the following questions:

- What made it easy or difficult to ask these interview questions?
- How comfortable were you in asking follow-up questions when you wanted additional information?
- To what extent have you set up a future working relationship with the person you interviewed?
- What else can we do to help you anticipate issues when dealing with other employees you are likely to meet in the near future?

Jigsaw Learning, Teaching Learning Teams, Teaching Projects

Jigsaw learning or teaching learning teams involves learners in study groups who concentrate on different information. Following the study of specific information, participants re-form in groups to teach each other. Use Tool 5.1 as a guide to write instructions for this type of activity. This is a perfect activity for repurposing existing materials. As you review the existing materials, decide how to divide the content into assignments for different team members. Use Exhibit 6.3 as a guide to write instructions for each team member.

Exhibit 6.3. Sample Team Teaching Project Instructions

Team Composition: There are six members of this study team. Each member has received material about one best-selling product. You will have two hours to study and further research this product. At the end of that time, you will teach the other five members of your team what you have learned about this product.

Product Questions: Be sure your presentation answers these questions:

- What are the key features and benefits of this product?
- Describe the customer who most often buys this product.
- What makes this product one of our top sellers?
- What are the major objections customers voice when deciding not to buy this product? How can you answer these objections?

Following the team presentations, ask the debriefing questions in Tool 6.10 of each team.

Tool 6.10. Jigsaw Learning/Team Teaching Debriefing Questions

Learners to Share and Interpret Their Reactions to the Activity

- What happened during your two hours of preparation for your presentation to your team?

- What was easy about this preparation? Difficult?

- What did you notice/observe about all the team presentations? How was that significant?

- How do these product presentations fit together?

Learners to Identify Concepts from Their Reactions

- How do these team teaching sessions relate to other parts of the selling process?

- What might we conclude from that?

- What did you learn/relearn?

- What processes/steps are similar to each of the presentations?

- What's important to remember about this team teaching project?

Learners to Apply Concepts to Their Situation

- How can you use what you learned from this team teaching activity?

- What is the value of this information to your job?

- What would be the consequence of preparing or not preparing this type of information about our products?

- What shortcuts can you use to help learn more about our products?

Polling

When polling, learners respond to a variety of choices through selecting or sequencing choices. Polling is also a useful tool in any training room to give the trainer feedback or to gain a sense of the progress of the group. Because of the technology, it is easier for a course designer to insert polling questions in online classes. When writing polling options, offer no more than four choices. Beyond that and the options become confusing for most learners. Writing polling questions is similar to the process of writing test questions, which is covered in Chapter 10.

Task Force Projects

Learner groups generate plans that can be used in the actual work situation to solve a real problem. There are four types of action plans, shown here in Exhibits 6.4 through 6.7. Exhibit 6.4 is an action plan that asks participants to identify what they plan to do and when they plan to do each task following the workshop. Copies of this type of action plan can be sent to the participants two months following the class as a reminder to assess how their plans have worked out.

Exhibit 6.5 is a behavioral skill action plan that encourages participants to plan *how* they will use the skills learned in the workshop. It helps them to apply a process learned in the workshop to a real-world problem, as well as to determine how to assess their success in using the new skill.

Exhibit 6.6 is a worksheet action plan that directs the participants to review specific pages in the workshop handout material, select an objective concerning the material, and then identify the action to take to reach the objective. Participants are asked to identify their level of achievement and when actions will be taken.

Exhibit 6.7 reviews the tools taught in the workshop and ask the participants to identify how the new tools can be used as well as how the participants' supervisor can help support and reinforce the new skills.

Exhibit 6.4. Sample Action Plan

Course Name: _____

Participant's Name: _____

Dates of Training: _____

Action Items	Start to Implement		
	Within Two Months	After Two Months	As Assessed

Exhibit 6.5. Sample Behavioral Skill Action Plan

State the problem you will be trying to solve:

Based on the information covered in the workshop, what steps will you take to deal with this problem? (List dates for each step in the margin.)

1.

2.

3.

4.

5.

6.

How will you know if your problem solving has been effective?

Exhibit 6.6. Sample Action Plan Worksheet

Complete the following objectives and actions for each area below. Refer to the appropriate page from your workbook.

Page	Objective	Action	Level	Date
4				
12				
22				
35				

Exhibit 6.7. Sample Supervisor's Help Action Plan

Tools I feel okay about and want to use:

1.

2.

3.

4.

How I plan to use them:

1.

2.

3.

4.

Ways my supervisor can support and help to reinforce:

1.

2.

3.

4.

Writing Tasks

Having learners reflect on their own understand of and response to training is an effective method to help learners transfer what is learned to the workplace. Learners usually write a descriptive summary of skills possessed or develop a plan to use new skills. Writing tasks at the beginning of a training session help learners describe an event or situation for which the skills to be taught will be applied. Instructions for writing tasks can be to answer questions, describe a situation or develop an application. See Exhibit 6.8 for an example of instructions for a writing task. This two-part example comes from a workshop about *Dealing With Difficult People*.

Exhibit 6.8. Sample Writing Assignment

Part 1

Instructions: Prior to the beginning of the workshop, write a description of events that occurred when you were attempting to deal with a difficult person. Make your description as complete as possible by telling the following:

- What was the setting of this confrontation?
- How did you feel during this event?
- How did you respond to this difficult person?
- Why was it difficult to respond to this person effectively?

Part 2

Instructions: Now that you have learned how to respond more effectively, use the four-step process below to write how you could have responded to this difficult person:

Step 1: Describe the other person's behavior,

Step 2: Explain your reaction to this person's behavior,

Step 3: State how you would prefer this person to treat you differently,

Step 4: Describe the consequences if the other person does or does not treat you differently.

What do you think the results would have been if you had used these four steps?

How comfortable would you feel using this four-step process?

What could help you become more comfortable in dealing with difficult people?

Session Starters and Energizers

Session starters are brief activities to bring the learners into the content through participating in a puzzle, question, discussion, or other activity. Session starters are effective when they: (1) are related to the content of the training, (2) low risk, and (3) involve everyone. Session starters differ from "energizers" because the purpose of an energizer is to create movement, rather than focus on the content of the session to follow. If a session starter is not related to the content of the workshop, high-task learners will judge the workshop a waste of time. If a session starter is high risk, learners will shut down and refuse to participate. Writing a session starter that involves everyone demonstrates that this workshop requires active learning by doing rather than learning through listening or watching others. Exhibits 6.9 and 6.10 are examples of session starters that meet the three criteria. Exhibit 6.9 is for a visual problem-solving session. This type of session starter would be appropriate for a problem-solving workshop or a workshop where you want learners to challenge assumptions, look beyond the obvious, or have a rationale for their choices. Exhibit 6.10 is appropriate when you want to honor different learning styles, teach about different learning styles, or honor different methods of solving problems.

Exhibit 6.9. Sample Visual Problem-Solving Activity

Show this problem on the screen:

Which number is least like the others? Why?

1. Three
2. Thirteen
3. Thirty-one

The correct answer is "number 2" because it is the only even number. Number 1 and number 3, and the words three, thirteen, and thirty-one are all odd numbers. Use these questions to debrief the activity:

- What made it difficult to solve this problem?
- What did you see?
- What assumptions did you make?
- How can you apply what you have learned from this puzzle?

Exhibit 6.10. Sample Kinesthetic Problem-Solving Activity

Show learners these instructions on the screen: put together a set of ten coins (or objects) so they look like this:

Invert this pyramid by only moving three coins.
This is the solution to the puzzle:

Here's the answer...

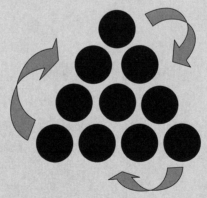

Used with permission from The Training Clinic

Debriefing Questions

- What made it easy to solve this problem?

- Did you move the coins until you solved the puzzle?

- How can you use what you have learned by solving this puzzle?

Next Steps

This chapter has explored how to write different training activities that are aimed at achieving objectives that are a combination of increasing knowledge, acquiring skills, and influencing attitudes. The next three chapters explore how to write additional learning activities that only meet one or two types of objectives.

7

Develop Learning Activities to Acquire Knowledge

This chapter will help the developer create materials for different learning activities to inform the learner, such as:

- Lecture

- Learning tournaments

- Self-study materials, printed resources, and information search

- Course pre-work

- Study groups

- Observation, field trips, and video

- Demonstrations

- Tests

Tools

- 7.1. Knowledge Methods Template

- 7.2. Observation Worksheet Template

Exhibits

- 7.1. Sample Learning Tournament Rules and Questions
- 7.2. Sample Information Search Activity
- 7.3. Sample Pre-Work Assignment Letter
- 7.4. Sample Demonstration Checklist

Lecture

In reviewing the Best Learning Experiences (Tool 4.1), we find several training methods that focus on increasing the learners' knowledge of a topic. The training technique used most often is the lecture method. There are several other techniques in this chapter that can be used as an alternative to lecture and meet the learning objective of acquiring knowledge. Use the template in Tool 7.1 as a guide to develop materials for each of these training methods to acquire knowledge. This template is a modified version of Tool 5.1. Tool 7.1 uses the lecture method as an example. Specific information about writing other knowledge activities follows the tool.

Tool 7.1. Knowledge Methods Template

1. Identify the business need that these materials will meet. How will you build a partnership with the learners' management?

2. Identify the class: What is the primary focus of the program? What is the time limit of the class, if any?

3. Identify the target population: Who will be attending the program? How many at a time? Will different levels attend the class at the same time?

4. Write the learning objective: What do you want the learners to be able to do by the end of the session? Review the verbs in Exhibit 2.1 to be sure your objective is specific.

5. Decide *how* you will evaluate whether learning objectives are reached. The specific verb in the learning objective can help you decide which evaluation tool is appropriate.

6. Select the delivery medium (classroom training, online learning, blended mediums, etc.).

7. Find existing materials that can be adapted or modified. If none exist, brainstorm content ideas using either a linear format (Tool 3.1) or a mind map format (Tool 3.2). Sequence the ideas. Begin to write your ideas with a statement of purpose. Free-write each idea and then edit your materials using "big picture," "what's the point," and "detail" revisions. Check the readability of the materials using an average sentence length of fourteen to sixteen words per sentence and 150 syllables per one hundred words.

8. Complete Step 1 of the five steps of adult learning by writing instructions to the learners on how to set up the activity, including what the learners will do following the activity, why they are completing the activity, and how they will do that. For example, "You will be able to identify five types of

cleaning products we manufacture" (*what* the learner will do following the activity). "You will be able to locate five types of cleaning products we manufacture" (*why* learners are listening to this lecture). "You will listen to a brief lecture accompanied by slides and programmed notes" (*how* the learner will do this activity).

9. Step 2 of the five steps of adult learning is the learning activity: lecture, learning tournament, self-study materials, etc.

10. Complete Steps 3, 4, and 5 of the adult learning process by writing debriefing questions for the learners to answer. In our example, these types of questions would be appropriate:

- What made it easy for you to locate each item?

- What did you notice when you were trying to distinguish the differences among the five types of cleaning products?

- What key point did you recognize in how our products are stored that will help you locate any product we manufacture?

- How will you use this information when you begin work in this section of the warehouse?

11. Repeat Steps 1 through 5 of the adult learning process for each content piece of the class.

12. Use the DIF decision tree (Tool 4.6) to identify how much practice is required to learn this material so the task can be performed on the job at the required achievement level.

13. Use the Methods Variety Scale (Tool 4.5) to avoid using any activity for longer than 15 minutes. Break up lectures and self-study materials by asking the learners to respond to questions.

14. Write a knowledge test that demonstrates the learner understands and has achieved the learning objective.

Tool 7.1.　**Knowledge Methods Template** *(continued)*

15. If appropriate, write programmed notes for learner handout material and create slides that support major points of the lecture, self-study materials, etc.

16. Write a leader's guide for the person who will facilitate this lesson. More information about leader's guides is in Chapter 11.

Learning Tournaments

A learning tournament is a technique to review newly learned information in a competitive setting. Use the material from lecture, self-study, or printed materials and write questions for the learner or teams of learners to answer. Depending on the type of learning tournament, select appropriate questions: multiple choice, true/false, sentence completion, etc. For how to write different types of test questions, see Chapter 10.

Write the rules of the tournament. How many points are awarded for a correctly answered question? Is there a point penalty for an incorrect answer? If one team does not answer the question correctly, does the other team have a chance to answer the question? How many points are needed to win the game? Learning tournaments made up of competing teams are less threatening to learners than tournaments that demand individual answers.

Exhibit 7.1 is an example of learning tournament rules and questions. The learning tournament in this example uses a game board as the format for answering tournament questions.

Exhibit 7.1. Sample Learning Tournament Rules and Questions

Tournament Rules

Players and Judge: Up to five individuals or five teams of two or three players each can play the tournament game. A judge (non-player) may be selected to verify answers. The facilitator can also be the judge.

Deciding Who Starts: Each player rolls the die. The player with the highest number begins first, play proceeds clockwise.

Selecting a Game Piece: Each individual or team selects a game piece.

Starting the Game: Each player or team places their game piece on or near the **START** game space. The first player or team representative roles the die and moves the game piece the number of spaces rolled on the die. To remain at the new space, the player or team must correctly answer the question on the Question Card from the card stack. If the answer is incorrect, the player returns to his or her previous game space. If a correct answer is challenged, the judge or facilitator can cite the organization resource to support the correct answer.

Variation: If a question is incorrectly answered, the judge or facilitator can provide the correct answer, or the next player can answer the question and advance the number of spaces on the die, if answering correctly.

The Winner: The player or team that first circles the game board once (or a selected number of times, as determined by the facilitator) and reaches or passes the game space just before the **START** position wins the game.

Tournament Questions

Prior to asking the questions, identify the correct answers and note the organization's resource where the correct answers are found. This information can be printed on the reverse side of the question card.

- When was our organization started?
- Who founded our organization?
- Name four paid holidays our organization celebrates.
- Where are you allowed to park?
- Does our organization have a carpool or vanpool program?
- How does our organization's carpool or vanpool program work?
- Where can you eat lunch or take breaks at work?
- Where can you store personal items during work?
- Who is the head of our organization?
- What are our business hours?
- Who do you call when you are sick?
- Where are the restrooms located that are nearest to your work area?
- Where is the nurse's office?
- How long are lunch and break periods?
- Who do you call if you are going to be late?
- What behaviors can cause immediate termination from employment?
- How long is your probationary period?
- What award can you receive for above-average work performance?
- Who is eligible for life insurance paid by the organization?
- Which medical plan allows you to choose your own doctor?
- Which medical plan requires the least contribution by the employee?
- How long must an employee work here before qualifying for medical plan benefits?
- When is the weekly/monthly work schedule available?

Self-Study Materials, Printed Resources, and Information Search

Self-study materials, printed materials, and information search methods all use existing materials that were created for a different purpose other than as part of a training program. Tool 5.2 suggests ways to adapt or modify existing materials. The key point in Tool 5.2 is number 5, *write instructions and processing questions to set up the learning activity and debrief it using the five steps of adult learning.* Exhibit 7.2 is an example of instructions and processing questions to set up this type of learning activity.

Exhibit 7.2. Sample Information Search Activity

Objective: Identify five types of cleaning products we manufacture and where each is stored.

Instructions: Use the worksheet below and after each brand name, write the type of material this product is intended to clean, the shelf life of the product, and hazardous warnings about the storage of this product. Enter the section, shelf and bin number on the worksheet to identify where the product is stored.

Time required: 30 minutes

Resources required: Product catalog (printed or online), warehouse schematic

Product Storage Worksheet

Product	Intended to clean what type of material?	Shelf life in months	Hazardous storage warnings	Section, shelf, and bin number
Product 1				
Product 2				
Product 3				
Product 4				
Product 5				

> **Debriefing/Discussion Questions**
> - What made it easy or difficult to find the intended use of each product?
> - What is the importance of knowing the shelf life of each product?
> - What special storage considerations are suggested for hazardous materials?
> - How comfortable do you feel about how the warehouse sections, shelves, and bin numbers are organized?

Course Pre-Work

Four types of course pre-work assignments were described in Chapter 5. Let's take a look at what should be written to direct the learners to complete this type of assignment. First, draft a letter, memo, or email that welcomes the learners to the class they will soon attend; describe the business need for the training event; state the type of pre-work assignment and the reason you are asking the learners to prepare this type of assignment. The reason for pre-work assignments is often to save class time for high levels of learning, sharing ideas that participants have had time to consider, etc. Exhibit 7.3 is an example of a letter for an Effective Presentation Techniques workshop. Decide whether the letter would be better received if it came from the learner's manager or the course instructor.

Second, decide how you will determine whether or not the learners have completed the pre-work assignment, and decide on optional or substitute activities for those who do not complete the pre-work assignment. Will learners complete an activity, a worksheet, or a test or will they bring materials to the workshop. If participants do not complete the pre-work assignment, will you develop a generic example or case study? If the use of a pre-workshop assignment follows a rest break or lunch break, learners who did not complete the assignment can use this time to complete an inventory or other type of pre-workshop assignment.

Exhibit 7.3. Sample Pre-Work Assignment Letter
Effective Presentation Techniques Workshop

Workshop dates: June 1 and 2

Workshop hours: 8:30 to 5:00 each day

Dear Workshop Participant,

Congratulations! As someone who will be giving presentations to our board of directors, you are scheduled for an upcoming session of the *two-day workshop,* Effective Presentation Techniques. To make this workshop a productive and fun experience for you, you will need to do some planning. Please prepare the following and bring them with you to the workshop:

A topic for a 5-minute practice presentation—a topic of your choice that is something other than a work topic. You will have the opportunity to present this topic on the first day of the workshop. Here are some ideas to start your creative thinking:

- My favorite sport
- Coping with difficult people
- How to do or make . . . anything
- My first "public appearance"
- The biggest lie I ever told
- My favorite character in fiction
- What I want to be when I grow up
- You are what you eat
- My pet superstition
- How to handle stress
- How I spent my summer vacation
- Teaching your teenager to drive
- This diet really works!
- My pet peeve
- Why I gave up golf (tennis, jogging, etc.)

A topic for a 10- to 12-minute practice presentation—this one can be a work-related topic, a different non-work topic, or it can be a more in-depth version of the first topic. You will have the opportunity to present this topic on the second day of the workshop.

For each of the topics you choose, please plan the following:

- *A specific objective:* What do you want your audience to know or be able to do after your presentation?

> - *A basic outline of how you will present the topic:* We will be dis-
>   cussing a variety of ways to organize presentations in class so you
>   will have some time to refine your plan.
>
> In addition to the topics and a bit of planning, the only other things
> you will need to bring to the workshop are your enthusiasm, your current
> strengths, an interest in continuing to develop your skills, and a willingness
> to give and receive feedback.
>
> If you have questions or concerns about these requests, call me at
> [phone number] or email me at [email address].
>
> [name of facilitator]

Study Groups

Study groups are a form of independent study. A reading or research assignment is given to participants to review independently and then discuss
their reactions to the material to enrich learning in the group. Write discussion questions for the group to answer individually and discuss as a group.
Directions need to explain each group member's responsibilities. Study
group preparation is usually done outside of class time. Jigsaw learning is a
hybrid of study groups and was explained in Chapter 6.

Observation, Field Trips, and Video

Having learners make an observation, participate in a real or virtual field
trip (application sharing), or watch a video can be successful methods for
learners to acquire information. How much is learned and retained can be
enhanced by job aids and observation checklists. Tool 7.2 is a template for
use during an observation, field trip, or video viewing.

Tool 7.2. Observation Worksheet Template

Topic, site, or name of video: _____

Objective of observation/visit: _____

Key points to watch for:

1.

2.

3.

Debriefing Discussion Questions

- Which of the key points made this a successful example of the objective of the activity?

- What was the main point of the observation? What did you learn from it?

- How easy or difficult will it be to use the information learned from the observation?

- What barriers need to be overcome to make this information useful?

Demonstrations

Many materials developers and trainers think of demonstration as a method to practice a new skill. That is true of return demonstrations and skill practice methods that are discussed in the next chapter. Demonstrations are really a presentation of the process or procedure to use a skill. It is very much like watching a video or making an observation. Exhibit 6.4 is an example of a checklist that can be used during a demonstration. Notice that the learning objective is stated first, followed by background information about the demonstration and a checklist of behaviors to be rated.

Exhibit 7.4. Sample Demonstration Checklist[1]

Learning Objective: By the end of this lesson, the learner will be able to, given a recording of a real customer's call, correctly answer all questions and complete all required steps in answering the call.

Demonstration: You will listen to a customer service representative (CSR) at an appliance repair and service center. The CSR's job is to answer questions about the types of appliances your organization repairs, the cost of a service call, and when service might be available as well as to troubleshoot repairs in progress. The caller is an owner of a laundromat who is a "good" and recurring customer. Your task is to evaluate how well the CSR identifies the repair need that the owner is calling about and offers an appropriate repair option that satisfies the customer.

Skill Performance Checklist

Instructions: As you observe a customer call, complete this form. Rate each step or task in the demonstration using the scale below.

1 = did not complete this step

2 = partially did the step, not to standard

3 = did the step, completed the standard

4 = did the step, exceeded the standard

[1]Reprinted from *The Art of Great Training Delivery* ©2006 by Jean Barbazette. Used with permission of Pfeiffer, an imprint of Wiley. www.pfeiffer.com.

_____ 1. Greeted the customer appropriately, giving name and title.

_____ 2. Asked open questions appropriately to gain information.

_____ 3. Asked closed questions appropriately to control the conversation.

_____ 4. Gave correct information regarding troubleshooting.

_____ 5. Made appropriate acknowledging statements to the customer's complaint.

_____ 6. Did not promise undeliverable service.

_____ 7. Was courteous and polite.

_____ 8. Handled customer's negative reactions appropriately.

_____ 9. Used appropriate closing comments.

_____ 10. Completed the call within required time limit.

List any additional comments to improve the performance of this CSR when dealing with this type of call.

Tests

How to create tests is discussed in Chapter 10.

Next Steps

The next chapter discusses best learning experiences that teach skills.

Develop Learning Activities to Acquire Skill

This chapter will help the developer create materials to help learners acquire skills through:

- Practice and return demonstrations
- Role play/skill practice

Tools

- 8.1. Skill Methods Template
- 8.2. Practice and Return Demonstration Template
- 8.3. Role-Play Template

You have seen a template to develop knowledge activities. The template is similar for writing skill activities. Look at Tool 8.1 for an overview of the process to develop activities for learners to acquire skill. Notice that task analysis has been added as the fourth step in this template.

Tool 8.1. Skill Methods Template

1. Identify the business need that these materials will meet. How will you build a partnership with the learners' management?

2. Identify the class. What is the primary focus of the program? What is the time limit of the class, if any?

3. Identify the target population. Who will be attending the program? How many at a time? Will different levels attend the class at the same time?

4. Complete a task analysis of the steps in each process or procedure. Identify the difficulty of doing each step and set prerequisites for this training session.

5. Write the learning objective. What do you want the learners to be able to do by the end of the session? Review the verbs in Exhibit 2.1 to be sure your objective is specific.

6. Decide *how* you will evaluate whether learning objectives are reached. The specific verb in the learning objective can help decide which evaluation tool is appropriate.

7. Select the delivery medium (classroom training, online learning, blended mediums, etc.).

8. Find existing materials that can be adapted or modified. If none exist, brainstorm content ideas using either a linear format (Tool 3.1) or a mind map format (Tool 3.2). Sequence the ideas. Begin to write your ideas with a statement of purpose. Free-write each idea and then edit your materials using "big picture," "what's the point," and "detail" revisions. Check the readability of the materials using an average sentence length of fourteen to sixteen words per sentence and 150 syllables per one hundred words.

9. Complete Step 1 of the five steps of adult learning by writing instructions to the learner to set up the activity, including

Tool 8.1. **Skill Methods Template** *(continued)*

what the learners will do following the activity, why they are completing the activity, and how they will do that. For example, "You will be able to select five types of cleaning products we manufacture and secure them on a pallet for shipping to the customer." (What the learner will do following the activity: "You will be able to read a warehouse schematic to locate any type of cleaning products we manufacture.") (What is the benefit for doing this skill well: "You will practice reading a warehouse schematic, locate product, and build a pallet.") (How the learner will do this activity)

10. Step 2 of the five steps of adult learning is solving a case study, participating in a simulation or game, conducting an interview, practicing a skill in a return demonstration or role play, etc.

11. Complete Steps 3, 4, and 5 of the adult learning process by writing debriefing questions for the learners to answer. In our example, these types of questions would be appropriate:

   • What made it easy for you to find each item?

   • What did you notice when you were trying to locate each item on the schematic versus the physical location of each product?

   • What is the key point in how to place our products on a pallet that will help you safely complete this process?

   • What will help you do this job faster?

12. Repeat Steps 1 through 5 of the adult learning process for each content piece of the class.

13. Use the DIF decision tree (Tool 4.5) to identify how much practice is required to learn this material so the task can be performed on the job at the required achievement level.

14. Use the Methods Variety Scale (Tool 4.6) to avoid using any activity for longer than 15 minutes. Break up lectures and self-study materials by asking the learner to respond to questions.

15. Write a skill performance checklist that demonstrates the learner can do each step in the task appropriately and has achieved the learning objective.

16. If appropriate, write programmed notes for learner handout material and create slides that support major points of the lecture, self-study materials, etc. Identify the physical materials needed to teach each task.

17. Write a leader's guide for the person who will facilitate this lesson. More information about leader's guides is in Chapter 11.

Practice and Return Demonstrations

Practice and return demonstrations can build skills when they follow seeing a demonstration in a live setting or on video. Once a demonstration is seen, the learner needs to identify the steps to follow during a practice session. Provide the learner with a job aid showing the steps and skills. When observing practice sessions, use a skill performance checklist. How to write skill performance checklists is described in Chapter 10.

Other essential elements of practice sessions besides observing steps outlined in a job aid are asking questions, giving feedback and making corrections, and helping learners summarize key points. The course developer needs to write questions to help the instructor and the learner get the most out of a practice session or return demonstration. Tool 8.2 is a template for the developer to follow the five steps of adult learning when writing material to help the instructor supervise a practice session or return demonstration.

Tool 8.2. Practice and Return Demonstration Template[1]

- Set up the demonstration telling the why, what, and how.

  - Why are learners completing a demonstration or a return demonstration?

  - What is the benefit to them?

  - What is involved in conducting the demonstration?

  - How will learners complete the demonstration or return demonstration?

- Conduct the demonstration.

- Focus on each step of the process.

- Identify what a typical performance looks like.

- Identify exceptions and how frequently they are likely to occur.

- Allow the learners to perform a return demonstration.

- Give the learners feedback on the return demonstration using a skill performance checklist.

- Share and interpret reactions to the demonstration by asking questions like:

  - What was easy or difficult about this demonstration?

  - What helped or hindered your progress?

  - What did you notice when you completed the required steps?

  - Are there consequences for completing a step out of the demonstrated sequence?

  - Was there a turning point in this demonstration when everything came together?

  - What was significant about this demonstration?

Tool 8.2. Practice and Return Demonstration Template *(continued)*

- Ask learners to identify the concept behind the demonstration by asking questions like:
    - What did you learn from this demonstration?
    - What is the concept that was demonstrated here?
    - What was the main point of this demonstration?
    - What is it better to do?
    - What is appropriate to avoid?
- Ask learners to apply what they have learned from the demonstration by asking questions like:
    - How will you use what you learned from this demonstration?
    - What do you need to practice some more before doing this process independently?
    - What type of help would you like from your supervisor or co-workers to do this process successfully?

[1]From *The Art of Great Training Delivery* © 2006 by Jean Barbazette. Reproduced by permission of Pfeiffer, an Imprint of Wiley. www.pfeiffer.com.

Role Play/Skill Practice

A role play is a training method that allows learners to practice skills or to empathize with another's situation by acting out a prescribed role. The purpose of a role play is to *develop empathy* or to *provide skill practice.* Empathy role plays are intended to influence the learner's attitudes. These will be discussed in Chapter 9. Role plays discussed in this chapter are intended to be skill practice sessions. The most effective role plays are conducted in groups of three to build on the practice element. The instructor and/or peers observe participants and give feedback to promote learning and application of skills on the job. Skills practice in small groups can reduce the learners' risk from participating in this type of activity. Some trainers and learners have strong concerns about exposing their lack of skill in front of others. Next, see how to use the five steps of adult learning to write effective skill practice sessions.

Suggestions for Writing Skill Practice or Role Plays

Develop the roles and situation in which the practice will take place. Be sure that the situation is not so close to home that the focus becomes the situation and not the practice. Skill practice role plays typically need more structure than do empathy role plays. Five types of structures require different amounts of preparation by the learners.

- *Improvisation:* Participants are given a general scenario and asked to fill in the details.

- *Specific roles:* Participants are given a well-prepared set of instructions that state the facts about the roles and how they are to behave.

- *Replay of life:* Participants portray themselves in situations they have actually faced.

- *Participant-prepared skits:* Participants develop a vignette of their own.

- *Dramatic reading:* Participants are given a script to act out.

Determine the format for the role play using one of the following formats:

- *Informal:* A practice that evolved informally from a group discussion.

- *Fish bowl:* Participants practice in front of the whole group, which will observe and offer feedback. Observers can act as a help-desk for the participants.

- *Simultaneous:* All participants are paired or put into trios to practice.

- *Alter ego:* A person stands behind each player, whispering in his or her ear.

- *Tagging:* Participants in front of the group can be rotated by interrupting the role play in progress and replacing an actor. Actors can tag an observer to come in or an observer can tag out an actor.

Plan how to debrief or process the skill practice or role play. All or some of these techniques can be used, depending on the objective of the skill practice:

- *Observers:* One or more observers are given specific instructions about what to observe and how to give feedback.

- *Self-assessment:* The participants discuss their reactions to the experience.

- *Open discussion:* The group as a whole gives reactions and feedback.

- *Trainer observation:* The instructor gives feedback.

Tool 8.3 provides a template to use the five steps of adult learning to make the role plays you develop a success.

Next Steps

The next chapter deals with writing materials for training methods that are intended to influence the learners' attitudes.

Tool 8.3. Role-Play Template

Step 1: Write the objective or benefit to the learners for participating in the skill practice session. Write a description of the situation and write directions to the learners about how to play their characters. Typically, one learner is practicing a skill that will be used on the job while the second character is another employee or a customer. The third person is usually an observer. Identify how much time the role play will take so participants know how long they need to stay in character. Describe how the facilitator assigns roles and how much time is needed for the learners to prepare for their skill practice session.

Step 2: When skill practice is completed in groups of three, often the same role play will be repeated three times to allow practice for all participants. A skill observation checklist is used to identify what is done correctly and what skills require additional development. After each round, it is appropriate for the learner observing the skill to comment on what was done well and what needs improvement. This is followed by feedback from the person playing the character and then by the observer.

Step 3: Write questions to debrief the role play in the group as a whole that allows learners to share and interpret their reaction to the role play. Examples of questions are

- What was said or done during the role play that helped the situation?
- What was said or done during the role play that hindered the solution?
- Was there a turning point in the conversation? What was it? How was that significant?
- What was positive or done well to demonstrate understanding?
- What could be done differently next time to obtain a better result?
- Did you observe any unique technique or skill application?

Tool 8.3. Role-Play Template *(continued)*

Step 4: Identify the concept from the role play:

- What does successful skill practice look like, sound like?

- How can we avoid difficulties when using this skill?

- What did you learn from this role play that you want to remember?

- What are characteristics of successfully practicing this skill?

Step 5: Apply what you learn from the role play:

- What gets in the way of using this skill successfully on the job?

- How will you use this skill and apply what you have learned?

Develop Learning Activities to Influence Attitudes

This chapter will help the developer create activities to influence attitudes through:

- Empathy role play

- Inquiry-oriented discussions

- Self-assessments and inventories

- Behavior modeling

Tools

- 9.1. Empathy Role Play

- 9.2. Debriefing Questions for Empathy Role Plays

- 9.3. Debriefing Questions for Inquiry-Oriented Discussions

- 9.4. Debriefing Questions for Self-Assessments

- 9.5. Five-Step Template for Behavior Modeling

Exhibits

- 9.1. New Performance Evaluation Form Discussion Questions
- 9.2. Self-Assessment Inventory Example
- 9.3. Skill Self-Assessment

The training methods for you to develop that influence attitudes include four techniques: empathy role plays, inquiry-oriented discussions, self-assessments and inventories, and behavior modeling. Two of these techniques, role plays and discussions, are mentioned in other chapters. The description of how to develop role plays in the previous chapter has a focus of skill practice. Empathy role plays are intended to influence the learner's attitude. How to write discussion activities was mentioned in Chapter 6. The focus for developing *inquiry-oriented* discussions is addressed here.

Empathy Role Play

As mentioned in the previous chapter, a role play is a training method that allows learners to practice skills or to empathize with another's situation by acting out a prescribed role. If the purpose of a role play is to *develop empathy*, then write roles for each participant that will evoke the appropriate reactions. The most effective empathy role plays are conducted in groups of three to check for participant reactions to the situation. The instructor and/or peers observe participants and give feedback to promote learning and application to the job. Some trainers and learners have strong concerns and fears about placing learners in a situation that could be embarrassing. Appropriately preparing and staging role plays can also reduce risk for participants.

How the Five Steps of Adult Learning Are Used to Ensure a Successful Empathy Role Play[1]

During Step 1, set up the learning activity and write directions telling the learners the purpose of the role-play activity is to learn to empathize with another's point of view. It is helpful for learners to review your written instructions to prepare their roles. See the directions in Tool 9.1, a sample empathy role play. Next, tell the facilitator how the role play is structured

---

[1]Adapted from *The Art of Great Training Delivery* © 2006 by Jean Barbazette. Used with permission of Pfeiffer, an Imprint of Wiley. www.pfeiffer.com.

and how to assign learners the characters they will play. Determine how much time is available for participants to prepare to play a specific character.

Depending on the complexity of the various roles, learners might need time to rehearse or prepare for their roles. For complex characters, try having all the participants assigned to a specific role meet together for five minutes and brainstorm what approaches they might take. During this time, ask the learners playing the other roles to identify what they will do to keep that role realistic and decide how they will react to the person playing the main role. Also have the observers meet together and identify things they will look for. Write directions and descriptions for each role.

During Step 2, participants play their roles. Remind the facilitator to keep track of the time allowed for each part of the discussion. When time has expired, ask participants Step 3 debriefing questions, such as those listed in Tool 9.2 for empathy role plays.

The next step is to reverse roles. Tell the facilitator to return to Step 1 and reassign roles. For empathy role plays, participants will not need very long to prepare. Debrief the role play with Step 3 questions. Since there are three roles (customer, clerk, and observer) return to Step 1 again and reassign the final roles, again allowing enough preparation time. Once the final roles have been played, ask learners to share and interpret their reactions to what occurred in the role play by asking Step 3 questions.

Next, proceed to Step 4 to identify the concept behind all three of the role plays. What feelings were the clerks to empathize with? See the sample questions in Tool 9.2. Finally, discuss Step 5 and ask participants how they will use what they have learned through empathizing. Step 5 questions are also in Tool 9.2.

Tool 9.1. Empathy Role Play

Instructions: The purpose of this role-play exercise is for you to experience the customer's feeling of frustration. You will play one of three roles described below. When you are asked to conduct the role play, conduct a 2- to 3-minute conversation according to the instructions below.

Customer: You are looking for a product you heard advertised on the radio. It was described as a machine that slices and chops all kinds of food. You have been walking around the store and are unable to locate the product. You see a clerk stocking a shelf and decide to ask her/him. Be persistent.

Clerk: It is very important to finish stocking this shelf so you can leave work on time in 10 minutes. The last thing you want is an interruption. Do everything you can to get rid of the customer who is approaching you so you can finish stocking the shelf.

Observer: Your task is to watch and listen. Do not interfere in the conversation you will observe. Watch for signs of frustration and anger from the customer. What does the clerk say and do that causes frustration?

Note: We realize that this is an artificial situation and that you would not treat a customer as you are asked to for this role play. The more you act out your character's role, the better the learning experience for all of you.

Tool 9.2. Debriefing Questions for Empathy Role Plays

Step 3: Share and interpret the learner's reactions to role play:

- Was the customer able to get the clerk to do what he/she wanted?

- What emotions did the players display during the role play?

- What did you notice about the customer's level of frustration?

- What behavior on the clerk's part caused these reactions?

- Was there a turning point in the conversation? What was it? How was that significant?

- What is the consequence of the employee's behavior?

Step 4: Identify the concept from the role play:

- How do customers (others) expect to be treated?

- What disappoints or turns off our customers?

- How can we avoid losing customers?

- What did you learn from this role play that you want to remember?

- What does excellent customer service look like?

Step 5: Apply what you learn from the role play:

- What gets in the way of treating our customers as they expect?

- What can each of us do to improve customer service?

Inquiry-Oriented Discussions

When inquiry-oriented discussions are used as the learning activity, use the learning objective to determine what types of questions to write to help the instructor facilitate an inquiry-oriented discussion. Chapter 6 discussed three types of questions: open, closed, and follow-up. Keep in mind that the purpose of the discussion it to help the learners examine opinions and beliefs that may prevent them reaching a learning objective.

Exhibit 9.1 is an example of questions that will enable a facilitator to lead an inquiry-oriented discussion. The learning objective for this activity is: *By the end of this training session, the supervisor will be able to complete the new performance evaluation form to accurately rate a subordinate's performance over the past twelve months.* Because a form that has been used by supervisors for several years is being changed, there is bound to be some resistance. Use an inquiry-oriented discussion to help the learners examine attitudes and beliefs and come to the conclusion that the new form has merit. The inquiry-oriented discussion can influence the learner's attitude toward the changes by identifying the changes, the rationale behind the changes, and the benefits of the new form.

Exhibit 9.1. New Performance Evaluation Form Discussion Questions

Use these questions to prompt discussion about the new performance evaluation form. Suggested answers and follow-up questions are provided.

Q. What changes do you notice between the old form and the new form?

A. The rating scale has been simplified. The behaviors rated are specific and measurable. The employee is rated against a goal, not being compared to other employees.

Q. What are the benefits of the changes to you as the supervisor of the employee being rated?

A. The system is fairer and defensible since the behaviors are more specific. The employees are being rated against a goal, and they are not competing with co-workers for monetary reward. The rating scale is easier to explain to the employee.

Q. What reactions do you anticipate from your employees when they are asked to rate themselves using this form?

A. Some might be defensive; others may rate themselves better than my view of their performance.

Q. How will you handle differences of opinion over ratings of performance?

A. Provide factual evidence of my ratings.

Once the discussion activity is completed, write questions for the debriefing discussion using questions for completing Steps 3, 4 and 5 of the adult learning process.

Tool 9.3. Debriefing Questions for Inquiry-Oriented Discussions

Step 3: Share and interpret reactions to the discussion:

- What is your reaction to the differences between the two form?
- How has your job of rating subordinates been made easier/more difficult?
- What about the new form surprises you?

Step 4: Identify the concepts from the discussion:

- What is the benefit of rating employees against goals, rather than ranking them against each other?
- How can you integrate this new form into your weekly routine?
- What did you learn about your ability to evaluate your subordinates?
- What is important for you to remember about the new form?

Step 5: Apply what is learned from the discussion:

- How will you use this new form to build rapport with your subordinates?
- What are the consequences of setting this new form into use?
- Based on today's session, what additional help will make you more comfortable using this form?
- What barriers will you address that were identified by this discussion?

Self-Assessments and Inventories

Self-assessments and inventories, whether written by you or prepared by a commercial vendor, are a useful training technique to influence a learner's attitudes. A self-assessment gives the learner an opportunity to examine beliefs and values that impact work performance. If you make a commercial inventory or self-assessment a part of a workshop, be sure to adhere to the conditions required by the owner of the assessment. To use many commercial assessments, certification or qualification is required.

Here are some suggestions for writing self-assessments and inventories:

- List the criteria that explain the various dimensions of the assessment against how the individual will assess knowledge, skills, or attitudes.

- Identify the format of the questionnaire. It can be a written narrative, continuum, rating scale, or pretest.

- Determine what narrative the learners will write. For example, at the beginning of a workshop, list the learning objectives and ask the learners to list personal objectives or describe a current project that will be used during the workshop as an example of learning points.

- Write a scale to rate each item, as seen in "Assess Your Writing Skills" in Chapter 3, page 20 of this book.

- Write a scale of reaction to specific situations, as shown in Exhibit 9.2.

- Write a self-assessment as a questionnaire that can be used as a pretest for the content of a specific workshop, as shown in Exhibit 9.3.

- Write directions to take and score the assessment.

- Write each item to be scored in the assessment.

- Write debriefing questions for the facilitator who will use the assessment as a learning tool. These types of questions should also be written for debriefing commercial assessments. Tool 9.4 gives some suggested debriefing questions.

As with all one-way communications, test the inventory/self-assessment with the target audience before making it a part of a workshop.

Exhibit 9.2. Self-Assessment Inventory Example

Attitude Assessment: How Do You Feel?

Instructions: As you read each description, imagine yourself dealing with this difficult person. How do you feel? What is your usual reaction? Place the number in the blank that corresponds to your feelings.

5 = angry, 4 = anxious, 3 = frustrated, 2 = in control, 1 = calm

_____ A. At work, a support person asked you to donate to a gift for a co-worker. You calmly and politely decline. Now she is berating you, in front of others, for being cheap, stingy, and selfish. How do you feel about dealing with this person when treated this way?

_____ B. You are busy at work when an angry manager comes in, screams at you, and calls you "stupid" and "incompetent". He says you made an error that you know nothing about. How do you feel about dealing with explosive, hostile behavior?

_____ C. One of your co-workers is a true "know-it-all" and is frequently right. Today you need to use the new spreadsheet package to do an especially important financial report. She is the expert on the new software (as she is quick to point out to all) and you could really use her help. How do you feel about asking her for help?

_____ D. You have a major report to finish today. It will require at least an hour of uninterrupted time. You are planning to negotiate with the other support person to answer your phone lines for about an hour. This is not an uncommon arrangement in your department. Your concern is that she will agree to anything you ask—very pleasantly—but then she may let you down just when you need help. How do you feel about negotiating with her?

_____ E. You are in charge of the department holiday party this year. Plans are about set and you are telling the group what you've done. One of your co-workers, as usual, begins picking the plans apart: "That won't work." "It's too much money." "No one will come." . . . on and on. How do you feel about selling your ideas to this "wet blanket"?

_____ F. The office has become intolerably overcrowded with both people and "stuff." Several of you have approached the boss with ideas about rearranging the area. Storage space is available, and there are even a couple of areas down the hall that could become another workspace. The boss is supportive and recognizes there is a problem, but no action! He can't seem to decide to decide. How do you feel about dealing with his indecisiveness?

_____ G. You've had several great ideas lately that have helped cut down some tedious and repetitious tasks in the office. Today you overheard the office manager telling the director how *she* had "streamlined" the office procedures and saved huge amounts of time and money. How do you feel about dealing with this "theft of ideas"?

_____ H. One of your co-workers in your area complains about everything from the workload to the office temperature. Today she has been especially vocal about some of the new personnel policies. Yesterday she complained at length about the boss. The day before it was a problem with her kids. How do you feel about dealing with these chronic complaints?

Record your scores here:

A = _____   E = _____

B = _____   F = _____

C = _____   G = _____

D = _____   H = _____   Total Score = _____

Exhibit 9.3. Skills Self-Assessment
Acceptable and Unacceptable Pre-Employment Inquiries

Instructions: Which of the following inquires would be inappropriate for interviews?

	OK	Not OK
1. Are you married?	_____	_____
2. Do you have children?	_____	_____
3. Will child care problems hinder your job performance?	_____	_____
4. What year did you graduate from college?	_____	_____
5. May I see your birth certificate to verify citizenship?	_____	_____
6. Do you have a disability?	_____	_____
7. Have you ever been arrested? If so, what for and how many times?	_____	_____
8. Where were you born?	_____	_____
9. Do you own a car?	_____	_____
10. Are you a member of any unions?	_____	_____
11. What foreign languages can you read, write, or speak fluently?	_____	_____

Tool 9.4. Debriefing Questions for Self-Assessments

Step 3: Write questions for the learners to share and interpret reactions to the assessment:

- To what extent do these results accurately describe you?
- How consistent with your experience are these results?
- How do these inventory results surprise you?
- Which inventory results are significant?
- Do any of these results contradict your experience?

Step 4: Write questions for the learner to identify the concepts from the inventory:

- What is the benefit of knowing your level of comfort or discomfort in various situations?
- How can you integrate this new information into how you view your team?
- What did you learn about yourself that is significant?
- What is important for you to remember about these results?
- What areas of your work are most impacted by the inventory results?

Step 5: Write questions for the learner to apply what is learned from the inventory:

- How will you use this information to build rapport with your team?
- What are the consequences of ignoring this information?
- How will you use these inventory results?
- Based on these results, what changes will you make?
- What barriers will you address that were identified by these results?

Behavior Modeling

Behavior modeling is a training technique that presents a successful image or an ideal enactment of a desired behavior. The desired behavior can be demonstrated by the instructor or shown on a video. Behavior modeling is similar to a demonstration and can also influence the learners' attitudes about how using a new behavior can benefit him or her by achieving a better result. The developer can successfully influence the learners' attitudes by using the five steps of adult learning. See Tool 9.5 for guidelines to achieve the best results.

Tool 9.5. Five-Step Template for Behavior Modeling

Step 1: Write the *what, why, and how* of the activity. For example, "As you watch the video on selection interviewing, you will learn to ask appropriate questions to screen out weak job candidates. Following the viewing of the video, we will discuss the model and then you will have an opportunity to practice how to screen applicants for job openings in your department."

Step 2: Write directions to the facilitator with steps to show the video.

Step 3: Write questions for learners to share and interpret their reactions to the video, such as:

- What impressed you about how the manager asked the job applicant screening questions?

- Did the wording of the questions sound like questions you would ask? If not, how would you change the wording?

- What was the reaction of the job candidate to the manager's questions?

- Were there any awkward moments during the interview? If so, how could they be avoided in future interviews?

Step 4: Write questions to identify the concepts from the video model, such as:

- What is the benefit of asking the type of questions you saw in the video?

- What is important for you to remember about the model you saw in the video?

- What is the most important element of this type of interview?

Step 5: Write questions to help the learner apply what was learned from the video:

- How will you use this information to screen job applicants?

- What problems might you encounter when using this interviewing model? How will you overcome them?

- What are the consequences for you and our organization when inappropriate screen questions are asked of job applicants?

Next Steps

The next chapter discusses how to write activities that use training methods that provide information, build skills and influence attitudes.

Develop Assessments and Tests

In this chapter we will cover the following material:

- Why write tests?
- Do we need to test?
- Criteria for testing
- Skill performance tests
- Knowledge tests
- Test development steps
- Test reliability
- Test validity
- Skill performance rating systems

Tools

- 10.1. Skill Performance Test Checklist
- 10.2. Skill Performance Test Template
- 10.3. Skill Performance Rating Systems
- 10.4. Skill Performance Test Exercise

Exhibits

- 10.1. Sample Matrix of Job Elements
- 10.2. Questions to Measure Knowledge
- 10.3. Sample Item Validity Test

Why Write Tests?

The primary purpose of testing is to make sure the employee is learning by measuring the employee's performance of job-related behaviors under real or simulated conditions. Tests are developed after writing objectives to make sure the employee demonstrates understanding of new information or demonstrates the same behavior described in the objective. Tests show whether learners have successfully completed the given objectives of the course. By writing the test *immediately after* developing the course objectives, the course designer obtains several benefits. The test:

1. Is written to the objective while it is still fresh in the designer's mind.
2. Measures just the key points of the topic/course.
3. Does *not* have questions on side issues that might creep in.
4. Guides the writing of the instruction, acts as a map, and keeps the instructional writing on point.
5. Ensures that standards will match the objective, thus dictating the passing requirements for the module.

If your objectives are an accurate statement of performance, testing is a good method to measure the effectiveness of the instruction, the quality of the material, the learners' level of knowledge and skill, and how well they will do on the job (predictive test validity).

Do We Need to Test? Criteria for Testing

In determining what needs to be tested, begin by referring to the critical elements of the job. These are established when a job/task analysis is conducted. The tasks that should be tested are those areas that are

- Important to the job;
- Difficult to learn and if improperly completed will impact on major portions of the job tasks; and
- Tasks frequently performed on the job, so that they form a major portion of the job activities.

Usually, learning objectives are developed for critical job elements. To identify a critical job element, use the matrix in Exhibit 10.1 and identify tasks that have a total of two or three items marked.

Exhibit 10.1. Sample Matrix of Job Elements

Task	Important	Difficult	Frequent	Total	Test/No Test
Scheduling service repair calls	X	X	X	3	test
Complete a call back tag	X			1	no test
Preparing repair estimates	X	X		2	test

Test only those items with a total of two or three items marked. That would be the first and third items on the chart above. If you determine there is a task that is important but is not difficult or frequently used, consider constructing a job aid to assist the learner, rather than including a learning objective and test item on that topic.

Skill Performance Tests

A skill performance test requires the employee to do the task. This is done through a practical exercise or other testing devices that produce performance, such as case studies, simulations, and role plays. The employee is observed doing the tasks and a subject-matter expert assigns a mastery or non-mastery rating based on the final outcome. For example, many operator jobs require written performance, such as completing forms, writing reports, or doing computations.

Write a checklist of steps that describe the process for the instructor to rate the performance. A rating system is used to identify how well each step is done and whether the steps are done in the correct sequence. When the sequence is critical, the skill performance test is often called a "process test." When only the outcome or product that results from the steps is critical to judge mastery, the skill performance test is often called a "product test."

Knowledge Tests

Knowledge tests check that learners understand new information, rather than their ability to do a task or perform a job. These tests can be administered in either written or oral format and can contain a variety of objective questions with limited correct answers. They can be machine scored by an employee not familiar with the subject matter. The types of questions most commonly used are true/false, multiple choice, matching, and short answer.

Following is a list of examples for different formats for skill and knowledge tests.

Examples of Tests

1. Written post-test with objective or subjective questions

2. Verbal/oral test; panel interview

3. Hands-on exercise to demonstrate a skill, usually done throughout the workshop

4. Summary exercise or case study that ties together all skills taught in the workshop

5. Create product:

   - Fill out a form

   - Print a letter from a word processor

6. Discussion of ideas

7. Return demonstration

   - Complete a repair

   - Take an order

   - Answer a phone call

Test Development Steps

For each objective, develop a test to determine whether the objective has been met. In order to develop a well-written test, use the parts of the learning objective to guide the writing of the test. Use these steps to write a test:

1. What is the performance stated in the learning objective? Does the *performance* in the test match the objective?

2. What is the test condition and does it match the condition in the objective?

3. What is the level of achievement in the test item and does it match achievement in the objective?

Exhibit 10.2 lists six types of questions that test for knowledge. The purpose is shown and followed by an example.

Exhibit 10.2. Questions to Measure Knowledge
Multiple Choice

Purpose: test reasoning
Example: Which are legally permissible questions to ask of a candidate for employment?

    a. Who was your previous employer?

    b. What child care arrangements do you have?

    c. How old are you?

    d. How will you get to work?

Completion/Word Association

Purpose: test for specific, limited recall
Example: Name two subjects to avoid when questioning employment candidates.

True/False or Two-Alternatives Response

Purpose: Measure cause to effect, effect to cause
Example: All offers for employment must follow negative results of a drug test.

Essay

Purpose: Test complex ideas or a creative approach
Example: What is the basis for the legal and illegal wording of questions asked in an employment interview?

Rating or Ranking Scale

Purpose: rate opinions or values
Example: On a scale of 1 to 10 (10 being best), *rate* the following as predictors of job success. (*Note:* a *ranking* question would ask the learners to rank the importance of each item as a predictor of job success by giving each item a sequential number from 1 to 5.)

___ length of service on previous jobs

___ no employment gaps on an application

___ similar or increased salary in new job

___ attendance record

___ amount of vacation previously taken

Semantic Differential

Purpose: reaction or intensity
Example: Rate the following as important characteristics in a job candidate:

Punctuality

useful									useless
1	2	3	4	5	6	7	8	9	10

When writing a test, it is helpful if the test is appropriately worded. Below are eight sets of questions that can help identify whether the test question will help the student learn and whether the test question is inappropriately worded. As you read the examples, decide why the "better example" is more appropriate than the "poor example."

1. **Poor Example**

   The Motor Vehicle Codes for highway use are revised:

   a. Every two years

   b. Twice a year

   c. On an ongoing basis

1. **Better Example**

   Using the unpaved shoulder of the road to pass on the right of a car ahead of you is

   a. Forbidden by law

   b. Permitted if you're turning right

   c. Permitted if the car ahead of you is turning left

2. **Poor Example**

   When a wig-wag or flashing signal is operating at a railroad crossing:

   a. You must stop only if a train is coming

   b. You must stop, then proceed when safe

   c. You must hurry across the tracks

   d. You must slow down before crossing

2. **Better Example**

   When you hear the siren of a closely approaching fire truck and you are not in an intersection at the time, you should

   a. Pull to the right and stop

   b. Drive slowly until it has passed

   c. Speed up to clear traffic

   d. Stop dead where you are

3. **Poor Example**

   By law you must register:

   a. A car that sits on your driveway

b. An old car that sits on the street

c. A hobby car that isn't street-worthy

3. Better Example

A sign that reads "WRONG WAY" means:

a. A lane to use when you miss the proper turnoff

b. A lane to use for reversing your direction

c. An immediate stop, as you are going the wrong way against traffic

4. Poor Example

Under the "Implied Consent" law:

a. You are presumed to have given your consent to a chemical test of the alcohol in your body whenever you use the highway.

b. You must take the test only after you have sought advice of counsel.

c. You only take the test if an accident has occurred.

4. Better Example

When parking a car headed downhill on a two-way street, the front wheels should be

a. Turned to the right, against the curb

b. Turned to the left, away from the curb

c. Parallel to the curb

5. Poor Example

The speed limit for passenger autos in California is

a. 45 MPH

b. 65 MPH

c. 55 MPH

5. **Better Example**

A pedestrian has the right of way at a corner:

    a. Only when a crosswalk is marked

    b. Whether or not a crosswalk is marked

    c. Only when the corner is signal-controlled

6. **Poor Example**

A yellow upside-down triangular shape means

    a. School crossing

    b. Stop. You are going against traffic.

    c. Let cross traffic go by first.

6. **Better Example**

The sign to the right means:

    a. No pedestrians permitted

    b. No parking this side of street

    c. Let cross traffic go first

    d. No passing

7. **Poor Example**

If you reach a corner and another car reaches the same corner from another direction and you can't decide which of you arrived in which order, you should yield to

    a. The car on your left.

    b. The car on your right.

    c. No one. Take the right of way.

7. **Better Example**

When you reach a corner at the same time as another car coming from a cross-street, you should yield right of way to

    a. The car on your right

    b. The car on your left

    c. Neither car, you have the right of way

8. Poor Example

Persons walking on the highway where there are no sidewalks should

    a. Walk on the wild side

    b. Walk on by

    c. Walk on the side facing oncoming traffic

8. Better Example

Driving so slowly as to interfere with the normal or reasonable flow of traffic, except when necessary for safety, is

    a. A violation of the law

    b. The right of any driver

    c. Legal but not advisable

To summarize, use these criteria for writing objective tests. The numbers correspond with the examples above.

1. Test for something of consequence.

2. Include repeated statements such as "you must" in the stem, so the point of distinction is clearer.

3. Don't give away an answer with grammatical construction.

4. Keep choices of equal length. Often we include more information in the right answer.

5. Test for reasoning, not fact recall.

6. Use a sign or symbol to clarify what is being asked.

7. When the stem is too long, it is less clear.

8. This one is fun; however, we want to offer credible questions.

Test Reliability

Test reliability means that a test consistently produces the same results. A test may be reliable but not valid. Therefore, both attributes must be established. There are four types of test reliability:

1. *Test-retest* reliability/test-retest mastery classification refers to the fact that a reliable test should yield the same or similar scores for a group of students if given again. This is determined by undertaking a study involving two administrations of the test.

2. *Alternative* forms reliability means that taking one version of the test will result in basically the same score as taking another version. This is important if two or more variations of a test are to be used (for example, through random selection of test items or parallel test versions), then alternative forms reliability must be established. The study often involves administering the test variations to the same group and correlating the scores, although more complex designs exist.

3. *Internal consistency or split-half reliability* asks similar questions to measure the same knowledge twice in the same test. This method requires that test items be deliberately sorted into two halves that cover the same material. The answers to each set of questions are compared. The degree to which the scores are similar determines the test's reliability. This is one of the easiest and fastest methods to determine reliability because it can be done during one test administration.

4. *Scorer/rater* reliability, also known as inter-rater reliability, is an issue when multiple judges score a performance test (for example, customer service personnel are evaluated in handling a test call). If the judges are appropriately trained and the administration and scoring instructions are clear, then each judge should give approximately the same score for the same performance. If the scores are not consistent, then inter-rater reliability is low and revisions need to be made.

Test Validity

Validity is established if the test measures what it claims to for the group you plan to measure. There are five types of validity:

1. *Face* validity simply means that the test makes sense to the test-taker. Face validity is generally guaranteed if the test item matches the objective. It is measured by asking the learners for their opinion of the test.

2. *Content* validity indicates the degree to which the test measures the achievement of objectives (job knowledge and skills). It is determined by expert judgment regarding the test construction practices. A *consensus* needs to be reached among a panel of experts brought in to review the test development practice and test items. This consensus should include whether or not:

   • The item tests a legitimate job-related knowledge or skill.

   • Performance called for by the item matches that called for by the job.

   • Test-taking conditions match the job performance requirement.

   • The item exhibits characteristics proper for the test type.

3. *Criterion* validity indicates the degree to which the test correctly classified masters and non-masters. Calculation of a "Phi correlation coefficient" on test data obtained from administering the test to a group of known masters/non-masters is performed. Proper classification of these test takers is critical to the success of this study.

4. *Predictive* validity indicates the degree to which success or failure on a test is predictive of success or failure on another measure (for example, performance that is measured in the future). With a criterion-referenced test (CRT), correlation may not be a good statistic to use to verify predictive validity if there is an absence of variance in the test scores. Expectancy tables and studies to obtain data may be more appropriate means to look for predictive validity with CRTs.

5. *Construct* validity shows the degree to which a test measures a quality or attribute such as analytic ability, integrity, or honesty. A construct can be defined as a non-observable trait hypothesized to explain behavior. A number of independent studies would have to be undertaken to establish construct validity for a test instrument.

How to Establish Validity for a Test: Item Analysis

When scoring a multiple-choice test, look at the number of responses for each option. This can help to determine whether the test is appropriately worded. Look at the information in Exhibit 10.3 and identify which questions (test items) may lack validity and need to be reworded. The numbers below each response are the number of participants who selected each option. The correct answer is in boldface print. In a "normal" test, additional information would be provided to the student to figure out the answers. That information is not provided here; just the results of the item analysis.

Exhibit 10.3. Sample Item Validity Test

Question Number	Number Selecting Option A	Number Selecting Option B	Number Selecting Option C"	Number Selecting Option D
1	1	5	3	**25**
2	3	1	2	**27**
3	0	**31**	1	2
4	1	**16**	10	5
5	**16**	10	2	3
6	2	1	1	**30**

Analyzing the Data for Validity

Review Exhibit 10.3. Which test questions appear to have validity? In Questions 2, 3, and 6, learners selected the correct answer most of the time so it would appear to be valid. Which test questions may not have validity?

Questions 1, 4, and 5 may not be valid because in Question 1, five learners selected an incorrect option. In Questions 4 and 5, half of the learners selected an incorrect option. To make these options more valid, look at the wording of the incorrect options and decide whether the test question and/or the options to answer the question need to be revised or whether a portion of the course needs to be revised or the course was not well taught?

Skill Performance Rating Systems

A skill performance test assumes knowledge and asks the learner to "do" the task that has been learned. The activity measured by the test needs to closely match the task described in the learning objective and also closely match the task done on the job.

Tool 10.1 shows the suggested steps to write skill performance tests.

Tool 10.1. Skill Performance Test Checklist

Decide what *type of vehicle* to use to measure the skill performance. The vehicle needs to closely match the job performance. Select a case study, role play, simulation, etc., as the vehicle. For example, will the learner who is studying to be a customer service representative be tested on how to answer a customer's inquiry by:

- *Case study:* Read a situation and answer questions about how to respond to the inquiry.

- *Role play:* Set up roles for class members who will pose customers' questions that must be answered. Often roles and situations are prepared and then acted out.

- *Simulation:* Place learners in a situation of responding to customers' questions without knowing what question will be asked and without a rehearsal.

Identify the *activity* that will be the subject of the case study, simulation, or role play. For example, will the learner who is studying to be a customer service representative be tested on how to answer a customer's inquiry by:

- Verbally answering a question (what form the customer is to complete)

- Complete an inquiry form (internal activity report)

- Write a report (summary of activity completed)

- Do a computation (how to compute an invoice amount)

Make a *checklist of the steps* for the instructor to rate the learners' skill. If the skill performance is a "process" and the sequence is critical, note that the steps must be performed in a specific order. If the skill performance is to produce a "product", note the criteria for a complete product.

Tool 10.1. Skill Performance Test Checklist
(continued)

Select a *rating system* for the instructor to measure the skill performance. Decide whether the rating system will measure:

- Quality (how well/correctly the skill is performed)

- Quantity (how often the skill is performed)

- Speed (how quickly the skill is performed)

- Sequence (the steps of the skill are performed in the correct order)

More than one rating system/category may be used. The "condition" in the learning objective often describes whether the skill is performed to a standard of quality, quantity, speed, or sequence.

Tool 10.2, a Skill Performance Test Template, is based on the four steps listed in Tool 10.1.

Tool 10.2. Skill Performance Test Template

Learning Objective (Record the learning objective that this skill performance test will measure.)

Identify the Level of Learning to Measure Skill Performance (Which one or more levels will be measured?)

- Application
- Analysis
- Synthesis
- Evaluation

Identify the Type of Vehicle to Measure Skill Performance (Which vehicle matches the learning objective and job performance best?)

- Case study
- Role play
- Simulation
- Computation
- Other

Identify the Activity to Measure Skill Performance (Which activity matches the learning objective and job performance best?)

- Answer a question
- Complete a form
- Write a report
- Do a computation
- Conduct an interview
- Complete a phone call
- Other

Tool 10.2. Skill Performance Test
Template *(continued)*

Write a Checklist of Steps to Measure Skill Performance (List the steps that achieve the learning objective and match job performance. Note whether this is a process or product checklist.)

Choose a Rating System to Measure the Skill Performance (Which type of rating system matches the condition of the learning objective?)

- Quality
- Quantity
- Speed
- Sequence

Tool 10.3 shows different scales to measure performance. Depending on the specific skill being rated, these scales can be modified appropriately. In all of these rating scales, the higher numeric rating is considered a better score.

Use Tools 10.1, 10.2, and 10.3 to answer the questions in Tool 10.4.

Tool 10.3. Skill Performance Rating Systems

Quality. A quality rating scale assumes there is an acceptable standard of performance. Consider these types of rating scales to measure *how well* or *how correctly* a skill is performed.

How Well a Skill Is Performed

1 = Fails to meet standard
2 = Completes few steps correctly
3 = Meets most requirements
4 = All steps done correctly
5 = Exceeds standard

How Correctly a Skill Is Performed

1 = Did not use appropriate people, tools, materials
2 = Skill partially completed
3 = Skill completed correctly
4 = Skill completed correctly under prescribed conditions
5 = Skill completed correctly under prescribed conditions and meets all standards

Quantity. A quantity rating scale assumes there is a minimum standard of performance. Use this type of rating scale to measure how often the step is done.

1 = Step is not performed
2 = Step is done once
3 = Step is done required number of times
4 = Step is done more often than required by the standard

Speed. A speed rating scale assumes there is a minimum or maximum standard of performance. Use this type of rating scale to measure how rapidly the step is done.

1 = Step is done too slowly or too quickly
2 = Step is done to standard
3 = Step positively exceeds standard

Sequence. A sequence rating scale assumes there is a standard order of steps for the process. Use this type of rating scale to measure whether the prescribed order of steps is followed.

1 = Prescribed sequence of steps was not followed
2 = Several steps performed out of sequence
3 = One step performed out of sequence
4 = All steps performed in the prescribed sequence

Tool 10.4. Skill Performance Test Exercise

Instructions: Use Tools 10.1, 10.2, and 10.3 and answer the questions below about the skill performance on the next two pages.

Does the skill performance test match the conditions in the learning objective?

What is the type of vehicle used to measure the skill performance?

What is the activity the learner is asked to perform to measure skill performance?

Is the checklist of steps intended to measure a process or product or both? Explain your answer.

Which rating system is used to measure the skill performance? Is the rating scale appropriate to the standard of performance on the job?

What would you change to improve this skill performance test?

Tool 10.4. Skill Performance Test Exercise
(continued)

Sample Skill Performance Test

Learning Objective. By the end of this lesson, given a customer's questions in a role-play situation, the learners will be able to correctly answer all questions and complete all required steps in answering the call.

Role-Play Scenario. You are a customer service representative (CSR) at an appliance repair and service center. Your primary job is to answer questions about the types of appliance your organization repairs, the cost of a service call, and when service might be available and to troubleshoot repairs in progress. You are about to talk to an owner of a laundromat who is a "good" and recurring customer. The technician who is on site now at the laundromat is a new field repair technician. The owner is upset with the length of time repairs are taking and the fact that the technician says two machines are beyond repair. Take the next five minutes and prepare to talk to this laundromat owner and provide appropriate information.

Sample Skill Observation Checklist

Instructions: As you observe the following role play, complete this form. You will be asked to give the CSR feedback on his/her performance. Rate each step or task in the role play using the scale below. Often the standard is given in the checklist item.

> 1 = did not complete this step
>
> 2 = partially did the step, not to standard
>
> 3 = did the step, completed the standard
>
> 4 = did the step, exceeded the standard

Tool 10.4. Skill Performance Test Exercise
(continued)

_____ 1. Greeted the customer appropriately, giving name and title.

_____ 2. Asked open questions appropriately to obtain complete information.

_____ 3. Asked closed questions appropriately to control the conversation.

_____ 4. Gave correct information regarding troubleshooting.

_____ 5. Made appropriate acknowledging statements to the customer's complaint.

_____ 6. Did not promise undeliverable service.

_____ 7. Was courteous and polite.

_____ 8. Handled customer's negative reactions appropriately.

_____ 9. Used appropriate closing comments.

_____ 10. Completed the call within required time limit.

Give any additional comments that could improve the performance of this CSR when dealing with this type of call.

Next Steps

The next type of materials for the course developer to write is the lesson plan. Chapter 11 offers information about three types of lesson plans.

11

Develop a Lesson Plan or Leader's Guide

This chapter will help the developer to:

- Develop contents of lesson plans
- Create scripted, outline, and overview lesson plans
- Assess which type of plan is best for a given situation

Tools

- 11.1. Lesson Plan Type Selection
- 11. 2. Checklist for Developing Lesson Plans

Exhibits

- 11.1. Sample Scripted Lesson Plan
- 11.2. Sample Outline Lesson Plan
- 11.3. Sample Overview Lesson Plan

Every lesson plan (or leader's guide) is intended by the course developer to be used by the instructor for these purposes:

1. As a guide or blueprint for an instructor to conduct training.

2. As a means of communicating the instructional strategy from the course developer to the instructor through learning objectives.

3. As a description/list of learning activities, time frames and materials required to conduct the training.

Contents of Lesson Plans

Lesson plans are considered to be complete and effective if they contain these ten components:

1. Why and how the course was developed.

2. A summary of target audience for whom the course is intended.

3. An overview of course content.

4. Special information about the course strategy.

5. Instructional objectives (also called behavioral or learning objectives).

6. Specific subject matter (content) to complete activities. The content needs to be prioritized for flexibility in presentation.

7. Description of learning activities, including practice and evaluation. (Check Tool 4.1. The Best Learning Experiences and Tool 4.6. DIF.)

8. Recommended time frames for each activity and breaks. (Check Tool 4.5. Methods Variety Scale.)

9. Transitions for each activity.

10. Summary of learning points.

Types of Lesson Plans

You will develop one of three types of lesson plans, depending on six factors. The three types of lesson plans are *scripted, outline, and overview.* A *scripted* lesson plan provides a written narrative for the instructor to use, complete lectures, and answers to activities. It is a verbatim transcript of what the instructor needs to say. An *outline* lesson plan provides learning objectives, a description of activities, and special notes for content explanation outside awareness of the instructor. An *overview* lesson plan lists learning objectives and activities with time frames and material required.

Use Tool 11.1 to identify which type of lesson plan is appropriate for any workshop. The amount of detail to include in a lesson plan depends on the six factors below.

Tool 11.1. Lesson Plan Type Selection

Instructions: Given a specific subject/class, rate each point on a 5-point scale or as directed for that factor:

1 = significant, 2 = above average, 3 = average, 4 = awareness, 5 = minimal or none

_____ 1. The subject-matter expertise of the instructor.

_____ 2. The instructor's knowledge of the adult learning process.

_____ 3. The instructor's comfort with facilitating groups.

_____ 4. The instructor's experience in customizing examples and/or answering questions about how to apply workshop information back on the job.

_____ 5. The need to have the content of the workshop delivered *consistently* at each presentation. (5 = great need/requirement, 1 = little need)

_____ 6. The choice for the participant to enroll in the workshop was made by:

   • The supervisor of the participant (5 points)

   • Joint decision of supervisor and participant (3 points)

   • The participant (1 point)

_____ Total points

Recommendation for lesson plan construction:

19 to 24 points = Use a scripted lesson plan.

9 to 18 points = Use an outline lesson plan.

0 to 8 points = Use an overview lesson plan.

Number 6 in Tool 11.1 is an issue for the developer who might want to state a rationale and benefit for including this content in a workshop. If a participant is a reluctant learner, he or she may not understand the business need for the training and why he or she was sent to this particular workshop.

See Exhibit 11.1 for an example of a scripted lesson plan. Exhibit 11.2 is an example of an outline lesson plan, and Exhibit 11.3 is an example of an overview lesson plan.

Exhibit 11.1. Sample Scripted Lesson Plan
Selection Interviewing Workshop

Note to instructor: Copy in italics and quotes is for you to say. Once you have the idea of what to say, use your own words to sound more natural. Reference items with a "V" are visuals, reference items with a "P" are page numbers in the learners' handout material.

Time	Objective/Activity	Reference
2	*Objective:* Give an introduction and set the learning climate by saying:	V 1
	"Many of us have been doing selection inter-viewing for years. This unit is designed to provide you with an update and perhaps offer a few new ideas. We encourage you to share your experiences with the group. You can tell us what works and what doesn't. We'll brush up on specific skills and review changes in employment law."	
5	*Activity:* Review session objectives on page 1	P 1, V 2
	"Please turn to page 1 and read the objectives listed. As you read, please circle the num-bers of the objectives that are of importance to you."	
20	*Activity:* Complete the survey of current skill level.	P 2, V 3
	"To begin, examine your current skill level by completing the survey on page 2. We will use this information to set individual-ized goals on page 3."	
	Allow time to complete the survey.	
	Ask participants to select three areas for personal development and fill out objec-tives on page 3.	P 3
	Summarize the objective setting by giving an overview of the workshop:	
	"At the end of this session, each of you will have the opportunity to practice your interviewing skills on tape. The items you have selected that require more skill	

development can be incorporated into your practice session. We will also discuss many of these items during this unit."

Objective: Determine employee selection criteria using existing job descriptions and performance standards.

5   *Activity:* Lecture: Preparing for the Interview   P 4

Lecture on selection criteria:

"How do you know what to look for? There are a number of tools that already exist within the company that can give you some assistance in these areas:

- *Review job descriptions.*
- *Review performance Standards for the position.*
- *Discuss operations, plans, and upcoming departmental changes with your supervisor (and perhaps subordinates) to ensure that, if the job is growing and/ or changing, the person selected has the necessary qualifications and interests to be able to change with it.*
- *Develop specific selection criteria which will assist you in choosing the best candidate. Begin thinking about questions which will assist you in determining the applicant's suitability (based on your needs). Remember: Selection criteria must meet two standards: (1) they must be job-related and (2) they must be a predictor of job performance."*

15–20   *Activity:* Read and review the job description   P 5, 6, 7
and case study.

Exhibit 11.2. Sample Outline Lesson Plan

Selection Interviewing Workshop

Time	Objective/Activity	Reference
1	*Objective:* Introduction and set the learning climate.	V 1
	For those who have been doing selection interviewing for years, this unit will provide an update, perhaps offer a few new ideas and review changes in employment law. Encourage participants to share their experiences with the group.	
5	*Activity:* Review session objectives on page 1	p 1, V 2
20	*Activity:* Ask participants to examine their current skills by completing a survey and setting objectives.	
	Allow time to complete survey.	P 2, V 3
	Select three areas for personal development and fill out personal objectives on page 3.	P 3
	Preview for participants that they will have the opportunity to practice their interviewing skills on tape. The items they have selected that need more skill development can be incorporated into the practice session.	
	Objective: Determine employee selection criteria using existing job descriptions and performance standards.	
20	*Activity:* Lecture: Preparing for the Interview	P 4
	Selection Criteria: How do you know what to look for? Use tools which already exist in the company:	
	1. Review job descriptions.	
	2. Review performance standards for the position.	
	3. Discuss operations, plans, and upcoming departmental changes so the person selected has the necessary qualifications.	
	4. Develop selection criteria that meet two standards: (1) job-related and (2) a predictor of job performance.	
15–20	*Activity:* Read and review the job description and case.	P 5, 6, 7
	Develop and discuss selection criteria for this case in small groups.	

Objective: Plan effectively for a selection interview through application screening and question preparation.

| 10 | *Activity:* Application review: Read through the list of items titled "Common Application Problems." Decide which conditions would prevent you from giving the candidate further consideration. | P 8, 9 |

Discuss in small groups and report to the large group.

| 10 | *Activity:* Distribute sample job applications to each group. Discuss the sample applications and identify positive attributes and questionable issues in relation to the information offered by the applications, based on each participant's experience. Use the Screening Applications Worksheet to assist the discussion. | |

| 10 | Have groups designate a spokesperson to report to the large group. | |

Summarize points to remember about screening at the bottom of page 7.   P 7

| 5 | *Activity:* Ask participants to read information on the types of questions. Discuss comments and/or needs for clarification. | |

Complete the questions on the bottom of page 10 in a large group discussion.   P 10

| 5 | *Activity:* Use page 11 to discuss the value of precisely constructed, deliberate follow-up questions that can yield important information. | P 11 |

| 15 | *Activity:* Assign two examples to each group of three to discuss. | P 12 |

Discuss reports in the large group. See instructor notes for suggested answers. Encourage students to record results on page 12.

Objective: Identify legally permissible questions to ask during an employment interview.

Exhibit 11.3. Sample Overview Lesson Plan

Section 1.01, Selection Interviewing Workshop (4 Hours)

Time	Objective	Trainer	Participant	Page/Visual
15	At the end of training the participant will be able to identify current skill level	Review objectives	Review objectives, set personal objectives, complete survey	P 1, 2, 3, V 1, 2, 3
30	Determine appropriate selection criteria	Lecture on four criteria	Compare criteria to job descriptions, discuss case study	P 4, 5, 6, 7
30	Plan for an interview by screening applications	List common problems	Large group discussion	
10	Ask appropriate questions	Lead discussion of how to prepare questions	Prepare questions	P 8, 9
30	Identify legally permissible questions	Review list of questions	Large group discussion of answers	P 10, 1
20	Avoid interviewing dangers	Lecture	Case study discussion	P 12
15	Make an appropriate decision	Direct discussion	Review materials on decisions	P 13
90	Summarize concepts to apply on the job	Videotape participants	Role-play interview	Video equipment

Tool 11.2 Checklist for Developing Lesson Plans

Instructions: For future reference, use this checklist to help determine whether your lesson plan is complete and will be effective.

❑ Background information on why and how this course was developed

❑ Summary of the target audience for whom this course is intended

❑ Select type of lesson plan to be developed (scripted, outline, overview)

❑ Overview of course content

❑ Any special information about course strategy

❑ Instructional objectives

❑ Specific limited content to complete objectives

❑ Alternative activities, prioritized for individualizing instruction or dealing with time constraints

❑ Selection of learning activities that are appropriate for the objective

❑ Description of learning activities

❑ Enough practice to develop knowledge, skills, or attitudes

❑ A means to evaluate learning

❑ Recommended time frames for each activity, including breaks. (15-minute pacing)

❑ Transitions for each activity

❑ Summary of learning points

Design Effective Visual Support

This chapter will help the developer create effective support through a discussion of:

- Criteria for audiovisual support

- Advantages and disadvantages of various media

- Use of flip charts and whiteboards

- Designing electronic slides with power

- Video scripting

- Converting classroom training to e-learning

Tool

- 12.1. Audiovisual Instructional Medium

Exhibits

- 12.1. Advantages and Disadvantages of Audiovisual Media

- 12.2. Sample Video Script Treatment

- 12.3. Draft Script Example

- 12.4. Script Writing Do's and Don'ts

- 12.5. e-Learning Script Example

Just as you can use the Best Learning Experiences chart (Tool 4.1), you can use Tool 12.1 to identify the best audiovisual support to achieve your learning objective. Tool 12.1 is a copy of Tool 4.4 and repeated here to emphasize the link among three types of learning objectives and the best audiovisual support. "K" is a knowledge objective, for learning facts, theories, or visual identification. "S" is for an objective that teaches mental or physical skill and includes analyzing or applying facts, principles, and concepts or performing a perceptual or motor skill. "A" is for influencing attitudes, opinions, and motivations of learners. Some support media are best used to teach only one type of objective. Others can be used effectively to teach more than one type of objective.

While choosing the best audiovisual medium can be guided by the type of learning objective, consider the following advantages and disadvantages of various mediums, shown in Exhibit 12.1.

Tool 12.1. Audiovisual Instructional Medium

Audiovisual Instructional Medium	Best Use		
	K	S	A
Audio recording	X	X	
Cartoons			X
Drawings and illustrations	X	X	
Exhibits	X		
Flipcharts, whiteboards, and chalkboards	X		
Models and mock-ups	X	X	
Music			X
Overhead projection, electronic slides	X		
Photos	X		
Printed material	X	X	
Real objects	X	X	
Simulators	X	X	
Toys			X
Video, film, and TV	X	X	X

Exhibit 12.1. Advantages and Disadvantages of Audiovisual Media

Electronic Slides

Medium

Advantages: Can change visuals, economical, realistic, different sound tracks possible, compact. Gives a consistent and professional look to visuals.

Disadvantages: Overuse of slides is not a substitute for delivery of content by other methods. Too many words on one slide are difficult to read.

Equipment

Advantages: Readily available, portable, front and rear screen, remote controlled or manual, controllable image size.

Disadvantages: Room lights must be dimmed to see all images well. Projection equipment is expensive and prone to theft if left unattended.

Whiteboard/Chalkboard

Medium

Advantages: Easily used, inexpensive, good for small groups, facilitates discussion, can be used by learners to brainstorm, etc.

Disadvantages: Messy handwriting, difficult for large groups to see, have to spell correctly, requires erasable pens.

Equipment

Advantages: Can be placed anywhere in the room, initial purchase not too expensive.

Disadvantages: Can be damaged by wrong type of pens. Surface is sometimes difficult to clean completely.

Video/Film/DVD

Medium

Advantages: Reproduces motion, instant replay, most other media can be used to produce it, special effects.

Disadvantages: Production costs are high, high expectations because of learners' experience with TV, need experienced production crew.

Equipment

Advantages: Still frame, slow speeds, easy handling, can be erased and reused, room can be lit. Cost is decreasing for players and can be streamed over the Internet.

Disadvantages: Production can be expensive, technical advances make obsolescence likely with some formats.

Flip Charts

Medium

Advantages: Diverse uses, good with small groups, facilitates discussion.

Disadvantages: Difficult for large groups and requires good printing skills, if learner's words are changed, learner can feel manipulated.

Equipment

Advantages: Inexpensive to refill, easy to post in room to keep agenda items visible to the class.

Disadvantages: Some rigid easel models difficult to transport.

Flip Charts, Whiteboards

Flip charts and whiteboards are good tools to make learning visual. Capture key learning points in different formats depending on the number of columns used to display information. A single list can capture brainstorming ideas or other lists generated by the learners. Two-column formats can chart advantages and disadvantages, old procedures and new procedures, etc. Three-column lists can include problems, causes, and solutions; current procedures, difficulties with the procedures, and recommended changes. Other examples of three-column lists are tasks to be done, who is to do each task, and due dates for the tasks; what information is needed, where to find it, and how to use it. As information is charted by the facilitator, remember to use the words of the person contributing the idea. If you paraphrase the contribution, ask permission to use different words and whether alternative wording captures the idea correctly.

Here are some design tips for creating charts:

- Choose bold colors. Black, blue, and purple are easier to see from the back of the room than red, pink, and orange.
- Lettering should be approximately 1 to 2 inches high.
- Use the fat side of the pen's tip when you write.
- If preparing the chart before class, leave a blank page in front of each prepared chart so the participants can't see through to what is behind.
- Add a border and icons to create unity and impact.

Lettering tips include:

- Use capital letters for headlines.
- Use lower case for details.
- Print neatly and clearly.
- Change colors to separate points.
- Use bullet points.
- Add stars for emphasis.
- Consider drawing lines between different elements or major ideas.
- Underline points for emphasis or when contributed by more than one person.
- Draw boxes to highlight main points.

Consider using flip charts to gather information about the learners at the beginning of a workshop. You can draw a continuum of years of experience and ask each participant to place an adhesive dot (or a dot made by a marking pen) to show his or her years of experience in a job, number of years in an organization, etc. You can write the learning objectives for a course on a flip chart and ask each learner to use three adhesive dots to identify his or her top personal objectives. To debrief this type of session starter, ask the learners to identify what the newly collected data says about their group.

Design Slides with Power

Try these ideas to give power to your visuals:

- Keep your visuals simple, clean (lots of white space), organized, and logical.

- Have a concise headline for every visual.

- Limit yourself to one idea per visual; include only items you will talk about.

- Add some color and pizzazz!.

- Follow the rule of five: no more than five words per line, five lines per visual; use the fewest words possible.

- Use upper and lower case; capitalize only the first word in a line.

- Use simple typeface, 30 to 36 points.

- Serif scripts cause eyes to move more slowly, so use for headlines.

- Sans serif scripts speed up eye movement so use for body of text.

- Shade darker to lighter as you look from bottom to top (earth to sky).

- Darker to lighter backgrounds move the eye from left to right.

- The best template is sometimes the simplest.

- Keep your message center stage, not the graphics.

- Organize the data to appeal to the audience, not the presenter.

Color Psychology[1]

People associate feelings and concepts with each color. In Western cultures, consider the following associations and uses:

---

[1]Claudyne Wilder and David Fine. (1996). *Point, Click & Wow!* Pfeiffer: San Francisco.

Color	Association	Best Use
Blue	Peaceful. Soothing, cool, trusting	Used as a background in over 90 percent of business presentations
White	Neutral, purity, innocence, wisdom	Use as the font color of choice in most business presentations with a dark background. Use as a safe background color.
Yellow	Warm, bright, cheerful, enthusiastic	Used in text bullets and subheadings with a dark background
Red	Losses in business, passion, danger, action, pain	Used to promote action or stimulate the audience, seldom as a background; don't use in a financial presentation unless "in the red"
Green	Money, growth, assertive, prosperity, envy, relaxation	Occasionally used as a background, but more often as a highlight color. Does not always turn out well as backgrounds when projected onto a screen

Transition and Build Checklist[2]

When creating a set of electronic slides, think about your audience and learning objectives to create transitions from one slide to the next and when building a series of ideas on the same slide. Consider these points:

- Is movement appropriate for this audience? How will they react?

- Has the audience seen electronic presentations before? If not, be cautious with the features you include. Remember that the eye follows motion. Too much motion may distract viewers from your message.

- What type of audience are you facing? What type of atmosphere do you want to create? Each audience and learning session calls for a

---

[2]Claudyne Wilder and David Fine. (1996). *Point, Click & Wow!* Pfeiffer: San Francisco.

different transition and build combination. Here are four common transitions and their effect on learners:

- *Wipes* and *box ins/outs* draw little attention to the transition itself.

- *Dissolves* create the impression of time passing and are used between messages or main points.

- *Fade through black* transitions are good for introducing pauses between major messages or prior to the summary.

- A *cut* is an immediate change to a new visual that is usually related to the previous one.

- Will the movement or picture contribute to the communicating power of your visual or are you adding decorative pictures and motions that will create a distraction?

- Have you included no more than three different transition effects and no more than three different build effects? Too many types of transitions and effects distract the audience.

- Have you varied your screens? Don't bore your audience with a build on every screen. Do not use builds for a series of simple ideas. Show all of them at one time.

Video Scripting

When you want to show a model of a skill or information about a product, a brief video can help the visual learner understand and see a model of the concept you want to illustrate. An essential planning step in creating a video is writing a script. Use these ten steps when creating a script for a video production.

1. Identify the reader(s) of the script and whether you want them to understand, do, or be persuaded. These are the jobs of most of the individuals who will use your script:

   - Director

   - Producer

- Casting director

- Actors

- Camera operators and other technicians

- Post-production editor

2. State the objective, written from the learner's point of view, not the reader's point of view.

3. Identify the learning points to develop.

4. Select the medium (see examples in the exhibits that follow):

   - Audio

   - Electronic slides

   - Slide-tape (or sound with images)

   - Video (slide-tape transfer to video)

5. Write the script treatment that gives objectives, setting, and characters who will deliver the learning points; lists benefits to the organization and the viewer. Effective treatments are best limited to one page.

6. Develop each character, with characters who are believable and whose actions are typical, unless exaggerated intentionally. Actors need to be representative of the company population in age, gender, and ethnic balance.

7. Write descriptions, dialogue, and directions.

8. Mechanical concerns to share with production staff:

   - Setting

   - One or two cameras

   - Camera angles

     - Wide shot (WS)

     - Medium shot (MS)

     - Close-up (CU)

     - Extreme close-up (ECU)

- Special effects (sound or visual)
- Keep the focus on learning
- Special edits, wipes
- Graphics, printed slides

9. Complete a story board with a picture/drawing of each visual.

10. Develop a cost estimate of production, duplication, and distribution.

Exhibit 12.2 is an example of a video script treatment for a Sales Skills Training program. Exhibit 12.3 shows a draft script example. Exhibit 12.4 offers some script writing do's and don'ts and Exhibit 12.5 is an example of a script for an e-learning event.

Exhibit 12.2. Sample Video Script Treatment
Sales Skills Training

Objectives: Demonstrate how the new accounts representative (NAR) can successfully sell a money market account. NARs often think of selling as order taking or something that used car salespeople do. This video is meant to be an attractive and easy-to-follow model of the four steps to the sale, illustrating enabling skills of listening and questioning, including how to handle an objection. The four steps include:

1. Identify Customer Need
2. Sell the Right Product
3. Close the Sale
4. Cross-Sell

The video is expected to be around 7 minutes.

Setting: Set at the NAR's desk in a quiet corner, non-distracting activity is overheard in the background. Two customers approach the NAR's desk (camera can follow the couple from the teller's window to the desk) as the NAR is finalizing opening a new account and is saying goodbye to her previous customer.

The couple waiting to see the NAR is in their forties and has just been referred to the NAR by the teller while they were cashing a check. The couple has just inherited several thousand dollars and want to open a savings account. They are not sure what is right for them. They want to earn as much interest as possible, but have access to the money while they decide on longer term investments. The objection will be for the small amount of checks (only three) allowed each month.

Cast: The NAR should be female and in her mid- to late twenties, neatly groomed, and dressed in a jacketed dress. The couple is in their early to mid-forties. Background people: person who leaves NAR's desk at the opening, referring teller, and others in the operations area.

Exhibit 12.3. Draft Script Example

Video	Audio
Wide shot (WS) shows teller line and branch activity in the background with NAR finishing up with a customer who smiles, puts papers in her purse and stands to leave.	(Light music under and fades after title branch music noise.)
Title over: FOUR STEP SALES MODEL	
(MS) NAR stands up and extends her right hand and says:	NAR: "Thanks for coming to Neighborhood Savings Bank."
(MS) NAR turns toward couple standing behind two customer chairs and says:	NAR: "Good morning. How can I help you?"
(CU) Man in pair smiles	Man: "Yes, the young lady at the counter said you can help us open an account."
(CU) NAR smiles	NAR: "I'd be happy to help you. Please sit down."
(MS) Man and woman sit down and man says:	Man: "My wife has just inherited some money from her uncle and wants to open some kind of an account."
(MS) NAR looks at man	NAR: "We have different types of checking and savings accounts as well as several other financial planning services."

(MS) NAR looks at woman	NAR: "Do you want to make frequent withdrawals or write checks on this account?"
(CU) Woman responds in a non-committal way	Woman: "Not right away. I just want a safe place to keep the money so we can decide over the next few months how to invest the money."
(MS) NAR reaches for brochures inside the desk.	NAR: "It sounds like safety of your money is important and the ability to earn interest while you decide how to invest it would appeal to you."
(CU) Woman nods in agreement:	Woman: "Yes. I think it is important to earn interest on the account so we can take our time with other investments."
(MS) NAR reaches for a note pad:	NAR: "I have just a few more questions before suggesting a specific account."
(MS) Man and woman nod in agreement	NAR: "How much will you be depositing to open the account? And, what do you estimate will be the typical balance while you are making your investment decisions?"
(CU) Man leans forward and in a confidential tone says:	Man: "Well the total inheritance is over $60,000, but we will only open the account with $1,000 today."
(MS) NAR hands a brochure to the woman and the man about "Neighborhood Savings Bank Insured Savings Accounts."	NAR: "Neighborhood Savings Bank has three types of savings plans that may be of interest to you. If you need to move your money sooner than three months, the term accounts won't meet your needs."
(CU) Man nods in agreement	Man: "Oh, I think we will be ready to make investment decisions before then."

Exhibit 12.4. Script Writing Do's and Don'ts

Make Sure Scripts DO:

- Start with a learning objective
- Make characters appropriate and realistic
- Help viewers easily identify learning points
- Use graphic support to identify learning points
- Identify benefits for the viewer
- Gain feedback and approval from the "client" before production begins
- Remain bias-free

Make Sure Scripts DON'T:

- Allow graphics and technology to obscure the learning points
- Use inappropriate language
- Use characters and situations that are not "too close to home"
- Use visual dimensions that distract from the learning points

Converting Classroom Training for e-Learning

In addition to the normal activities associated with designing training for a classroom environment like:

- Identify the target population

- Complete a task analysis

- Determine course prerequisites

- Identify learning objectives

Consider the following situations for e-learning:

1. The type of training being conducted lends itself to visual enhancement.

2. There is a large population to receive the training located in scattered geographic sites.

3. A cost/benefit analysis determines that e-learning is appropriate.

Here are some reminders when developing your e-learning program:

1. Find ways to involve the audience every 15 minutes.

2. Avoid "talking heads."

3. Provide visual cues on the screen to direct participants to the appropriate handout page.

4. Have a conference call with site facilitators to review the script and be sure they have needed material. Site facilitators are the "eyes and ears" of the broadcast team.

5. Conduct a rehearsal to refine the timing and coordinate learning points with the technical crew. Practice using equipment.

6. Use a variety of settings, video clips, discussion, interviews, etc., to keep visual interest.

7. Provide strong introduction and summary segments.

8. Have written directions in the handout materials, as well as state them during the broadcast and show them on the screen.

9. Review the content of the handout materials with the "client" to make sure all content is appropriate for broadcast.

10. Use icons in handout materials and on camera as visual cues for a shift in activities.

11. Plan for hourly breaks of 5 to 10 minutes.

12. Use a studio audience to get visual feedback. Use a two-way audio system to hear from participants.

13. Invite participants without audio to send questions by chat or fax if a question could not be answered directly on the air.

Exhibit 12.5. e-Learning Script Example

Phase 2: The Performance Consultant in Action—Wednesday, July 30

Time	Visual	Narrative
Event 1 12:00 5	Welcome Back graphic	Welcome from Jean/Diane Answer from chat and faxed questions about Phase 1
Event 2 10	PP build of page 29: partnership between manager and consultant CG "Page 29"	Jean and Diane discuss page 29 Address partnership question about how formal/informal is the partnership.
Event 3 5 10 2 3	PP build of four phases of influence: CG "page 30" Planning People Resources (budget) Need Diagnosis, CG "page 31" Show polling questions for exercise on page 31 PP of questions for values page 32, CG "page 32" PP of questions for beliefs and facts, page 32 Action, CG "page 32" Testimonial Research Reference Pilot CG "Page 32" Evaluation	Jean: Explain four points on page 30 Diane: Ask participants to answer polling questions to identify if statement is fact, belief, or value on page 31 Jean: Explain additional questions on page 32 Continue discussion between Jean and Diane for rest of page 30
Event 4 15	PP with directions to case on page 33 CG "page 33" and divides groups into breakout rooms. Countdown clock with 15 minutes 1-minute warning	Jean: Ask participants to complete the case study on page 33 Diane: Ask learners in Cincinnati, Detroit, Greensboro, Houston to be ready to give the first answer for Chief's point of view Memphis, New Orleans, Overland Park, Richmond, and Seattle for manager's point of view

12:50 Event 5 10 floor manager give Jean 5-minute cue	Jean writes on whiteboard with title for Manager CG "page 34" PP build of Unit 7, page 35 CG "page 35"	Diane: Ask participants to give reports from two perspectives Jean: Summary of influencing main points, including influencing ISTJ manager, page 34 Transition to unit 7
Event 6 5	Break Countdown clock 5 minutes 1-minute warning	Music
1:05 Event 7 2	Jean writes on whiteboard CG "page 36"	Diane: Interviewing skills are needed in the "explore" and "diagnose" steps Two types of interviews are assessment and benchmarking
Event 8 15 floor manager give Jean cue every 4 minutes 5	Diane on Set 2 (console) Jean and Larry on Set 1 (table and chairs) CG "Questions on pages 37-38" Diane shown in window when answering sites for more questions Diane takes calls (use window of Jean and Larry. Diane writes questions from participants) CG "page 39"	Diane: Explain how questions were gathered at the end of phase one from the participants Participants can follow questions on pages 37 and 38 Diane will ask participants to raise their hands after 5 minutes when most of the beginning questions have been asked for additional questions Repeat same process for the middle and end of the interview. Jean asks participants to raise their hands and tell us what makes an effective assessment interview. Participants can record answers on page 39 while Diane organizes speakers
1:27 Event 9 10 5	Jean interviews Tom as the Master performer (Set 1) Diane writes on whiteboard as participants contribute additional questions. CG "page 41"	Jean asks questions and Diane asks participants to raise their hands with additional questions for the beginning, middle, and end of the interview Jean asks participants to raise their hands and tell us what makes an effective benchmarking interview. Participants can record answers on page 41 while Diane organizes speakers.

Bibliography

Army School of Instructional Technology, UK Royal Army Education Corps, Pamphlet No. 2, "Job Analysis for Training." Army Code No. 70670.

Barbazette, Jean. *The Trainer's Support Handbook*. New York: McGraw-Hill, 2001.

Barbazette, Jean. *Instant Case Studies*. San Francisco: Pfeiffer, 2003.

Barbazette, Jean. *The Trainer's Journey to Competence: Tools, Assessments and Models*. San Francisco: Pfeiffer, 2005.

Barbazette, Jean. *The Art of Great Training Delivery: Strategies, Tools, and Tactics*. San Francisco: Pfeiffer, 2006.

Barbazette, Jean. *Training Needs Assessment: Methods, Tools, and Techniques*. San Francisco: Pfeiffer, 2006.

Barbazette, Jean. *Successful New Employee Orientation: A Step-by-Step Guide for Designing, Facilitating, and Evaluating Your Program* (3rd ed.). San Francisco: Pfeiffer. 2007.

Barbazette, Jean. *Managing the Training Function for Bottom-Line Results*. San Francisco: Pfeiffer, 2008.

Christakis, Dimitri. Early Television Exposure and Subsequent Attentional Problems in Children. *Pediatrics, 113*(4), April 2004.

Clark, Ruth. *Developing Technical Training*. Reading, MA: Addison-Wesley, 1989.

Josephson, Wendy. How Children Process Television. *Issue Brief Series*. Studio City CA: Mediascope Press, 1997.

Kirkpatrick, Donald. *Evaluating Training Programs* (2nd ed.). San Francisco: Berrett-Koehler, 1989.

Labin, Jenn. *Real World Training Design: Navigating Common Constraints for Exceptional Results*. Alexandria, VA: ASTD Press, 2012.

Pfeiffer, J. William. *UA Training Technologies 7: Presentation & Evaluation Skills in Human Resource Development* (pp. 66–68). San Francisco: Pfeiffer, 1988.

Wilder, Claudyne, and David Fine. *Point, Click & Wow*. San Francisco: Pfeiffer, 1996.

Websites

Gunning Fog Index. www.readabilityformulas.com.

HRDQ, King of Prussia, PA. www.hrdq.com.

The Training Clinic. www.thetrainingclinic.com.

About the Author

Jean Barbazette is the founder of The Training Clinic, a training and consulting firm she began in 1977. Her company focuses on training trainers throughout the United States for major profit, non-profit, and government organizations. The Training Clinic has three international licensees in the Netherlands, Hungary, and Colombia. Prior books include *Successful New Employee Orientation* (3rd ed.) (Pfeiffer, 2007); *The Trainer's Support Handbook* (McGraw-Hill, 2001); *Instant Case Studies* (Pfeiffer, 2003); *The Trainer's Journey to Competence* (Pfeiffer, 2005); *Training Needs Assessment* (Pfeiffer, 2006); *The Art of Great Training Delivery* (Pfeiffer, 2006); and *Managing the Training Function for Bottom-Line Results* (Pfeiffer, 2008). She is a frequent contributor to *ASTD Training & Development Sourcebooks*, *McGraw-Hill Training & Performance Sourcebooks*, and *Pfeiffer Annuals*.

Jean Barbazette, Founder
The Training Clinic
645 Seabreeze Drive
Seal Beach, CA 90740
jean@thetrainingclinic.com
www.thetrainingclinic.com

Index

Page references followed by *t* indicate a tool; followed by *e* indicate an exhibit.

A

Action plans: sample behavioral skill, 138, 140*e*; sample of, 138, 139*e*; sample plan for securing supervisor's help, 138, 142*e*; sample worksheet for, 138, 141*e*

Adapt or Modify Existing Materials tool, 66*t*–67*t*, 157

Adult learning model: Adapt or Modify Existing Materials tool used with, 66*t*, 67*t*; behavior modeling to influence learner attitude using the, 191–193*t*; empathy role play using the five steps of the, 179–182*t*; five steps of the, 68–72; use five steps to teach

application sharing, 92; Knowledge Methods Template tool used with, 152*e*–153*e*; Practice and Return Demonstration Template used with five steps of, 170, 171*t*–172*t*; role play/skill practice using the five steps of the, 173–174, 175*t*–176*t*; Seven-Step Process to Design Learning Materials tool used with, 63*t*; Skill Methods Template tool used with, 167*t*–168*t*

Adult learning steps, 179–180; step 1: trainer sets up learning activity, 68–69; step 2: learners participate in learning activity, 69; step 3: learners share and interpret their reactions, 69–70, 71;